99

(37)

YORKSHIRE'S WAR

Voices of the First World War

YORKSHIRE'S WAR

Tim Lynch

AMBERLEY

First published 2014

Amberley Publishing
The Hill, Stroud
Gloucestershire, GL5 4EP

www. amberley-books.com

Copyright © Tim Lynch, 2014

British Library Cataloguing in Publication Data. A catalogue record for this book is available
from the British Library.

ISBN 978 1 4456 3448 7 (print)
ISBN 978 1 4456 3456 2 (ebook)

Typesetting and Origination by Amberley Publishing.
Printed in the UK.

CONTENTS

ACKNOWLEDGEMENTS

At least four members of my family served in the Great War, all of them with Yorkshire regiments. My father, Albert, knew some of the people referred to in the coming pages, a reminder that a century only seems a long time but is barely more than a single lifetime. I grew up surrounded by veterans, but was too young at the time to really appreciate the wealth of history around me. I'm therefore extremely grateful that others took that opportunity and gathered the stories of the men who marched away.

In particular I'd like to thank Malcolm Johnson of the Western Front Association, whose work for the King's Own Yorkshire Light Infantry (KOYLI) museum has been extremely useful. Thanks too to Jon Cooksey, also of the Western Front Association and the Guild of Battlefield Guides, for his work on the Barnsley Pals and for his unfailing encouragement and help since the start of my writing career. Paul Oldfield's work on the Sheffield Pals has also been a rich source, as has David Raw's account of the Bradford Pals and Laurie Milne's on the Leeds men. The *Pals* series, published by Barnsley-based Pen & Sword, are probably the best starting point for anyone interested in the experiences of local men in the Great War.

Thanks to Christian Duck at Amberley Publishing for giving me the chance to write this and for being patient when deadlines came and went.

As ever, my thanks to my wife, Jacqueline, and son Josh. Special thanks to Bethany for her work as research assistant. Few teenagers regard trawling through musty old books for anorak dads as a good use of their weekends, but I'm grateful for the help.

1

THE ROAD TO WAR

A special issue of *The Times* on the evening of the 3 September contained the following vivid account – the first published – of the happenings in the town of Goole, Yorkshire:

Goole, September 3.
Shortly before five o'clock on Sunday morning the night operator of the telephone call-office here discovered an interruption on the trunk-line, and on trying the telegraphs was surprised to find that there was no communication in any direction. The railway station, being rung up, replied that their wires were also down. Almost immediately afterwards a well-known North Sea pilot rushed into the post office and breathlessly asked that he might telephone to Lloyd's. When told that all communication was cut off he wildly shouted that a most extraordinary sight was to be seen in the River Ouse, up which was approaching a continuous procession of tugs, towing flats, and barges filled with German soldiers.

This was proved to be an actual fact, and the inhabitants of Goole, awakened from their Sunday morning slumbers by the shouts of alarm in the streets, found, to their abject amazement, foreign soldiers swarming everywhere. On the quay they found activity everywhere, German being spoken on all hands. They watched a body of cavalry, consisting of the 1st Westphalian Hussars, the Westphalian Cuirassiers, land with order and ease at the Victoria Pier, whence, after being formed up on the quay, they advanced at a sharp trot up Victoria Street, Ouse Street, and

In the years before the Great War, stories of the invasion of Britain by German troops was a popular subject.

North Street to the railway station. Here, as is generally known, there are large sidings of the North-East Lancashire and Yorkshire lines in direct communication both with London and the great cities of the north. The enemy here found great quantities of engines and rolling stock, all of which was at once seized, together with huge stacks of coal at the new sidings. Meanwhile, cavalry of the 14th Brigade, consisting of Westphalian Hussars and Uhlans, were rapidly disembarking at Old Goole, and, advancing southwards over the open country of Goole Moors and Thorne Waste, occupied Crowle. Both cavalry brigades were acting independently of the main body, and by their vigorous action, both south and west, they were entirely screening what was happening in the port of Goole.

There are wild rumours [in Sheffield] that the enemy have burned Grimsby… It has been gathered from the invaders that the VIII Army Corps of the Germans have landed and seized Hull, but at present this is not confirmed. There is, alas! no communication with the place, therefore, the report may possibly be true … Dewsbury, Huddersfield, Wakefield, and Selby are all intensely excited over the sudden appearance of German soldiers, and were at first inclined to unite to stem their progress. But the German proclamation, showing the individual peril of any citizen taking arms against the invaders, having been posted everywhere, has held everyone scared and in silent inactivity… Away to the eastward of Sheffield – exactly where was yet unknown – sixty-thousand perfectly equipped and thoroughly trained German horse, foot, and artillery, were ready at any moment to advance westward into our manufacturing districts!

William Le Queux, *The Invasion of 1910*, 1906

The unification of Prussia, Saxony, Bavaria and other states into a unified German empire in 1871 had, many believed, created a serious threat to European peace and, more importantly, to Britain's status as a world power that could not be ignored. The Kaiser's open support for the Boers during the South African War had demonstrated his ambition to undermine British power in its overseas territories, and the widely reported supply of German weapons to Irish Nationalists intensified the threat of civil war in the United Kingdom over the issue of Irish Home Rule. For years, the public had been bombarded with lurid stories of German agents plotting Britain's downfall and, in 1906, when Le Queux's fictional account of a German invasion and conquest of England was commissioned by the *Daily Mail*, the paper began advising its readers that they should refuse to be served by German or Austrian waiters and to demand to see the passport of those claiming to be Swiss. Elsewhere, the million-selling *Boy's Own* paper advised its readers that German tourists in Britain were spies who could be identified by the jackboots they wore in bad weather, prompting an eight-year-old Evelyn Waugh to form a gang dedicated to drilling and preparing for invasion. In the first decade of the twentieth century, it seemed, going to war with Germany seemed almost inevitable. It was only a matter of time…

The county of Yorkshire, the prime target of Le Queux's Teutonic hordes, had seen huge changes over the previous century:

Between the Yorkshire of the eighteenth century and the Yorkshire of today [1908] stretches a gulf so wide that one can scarcely see across it … At the end of the eighteenth century, Leeds, the largest town in the three Ridings, could not boast a population of more than fifty thousand; that of Sheffield was about ten thousand less. In Bradford, a black, filthy town, intersected by a narrow beck, choked and polluted with refuse, there were only twelve hundred persons who were actually engaged in the staple trades, and the place was of small commercial value or rank. The older towns of the county, such as Pontefract, Beverley, Knaresborough, Richmond were mere market centres, unlikely to increase in population or wealth. Some idea of the remarkable development of the great Yorkshire towns during the hundred years which elapsed between 1801 and 1901 may be gained from the bare statistics of the census-takers and other official returns. The population of Leeds in 1801 was 53, 12; in 1901 it was 428, 68. In the same period Sheffield increased from 45, 55 to 380, 93, and Hull from about 30,000 to 240, 59. Bradford in 1831 could only number 43, 27 but by 1901 the population had swelled to 279, 67. Between 1821 and 1901 the population of Halifax increased from 14, 64 to 104, 36. York in 1801 had a population of 30,000 and had probably dwindled in size – so far as numbers are concerned – during the eighteenth century; the increase in trade of the nineteenth raised its population to 77, 14. But most marvellous of all developments in the matter of population is that of Middlesbrough, a town whose entire population was housed under one roof in 1820, and now includes sixty miles of streets and 91, 02 persons within its boundaries.

J. S. Fletcher, *A Book About Yorkshire*, 1908

By the end of the Victorian period, Yorkshire had become, according to one observer, 'a land of almost violent contrasts' with a rugged coastline, open moorland and the farmland of the North and East Ridings giving way to the industrial heartland of empire in the mills, factories and mines of the West Riding:

Bradford at the turn of the century.

Those who ride out of rural Yorkshire across the border of the coal field may well be pardoned if they experience for the moment a sense of bewilderment. Gone in a moment are the wholesome green fields, the pleasant country lanes and the quiet red brick cottages. Instead we have piles of accumulating refuse; dusty roads, with unspeakable surface; footpaths grimy with cinders and coal dust; long gaunt rows of unlovely houses, set down anyhow by the highways and hedges; scraps of walled yard instead of garden; monotonous lines of monstrous ash-bins; dirty children at play in the street; everywhere misery, filth and squalor. It is difficult to believe that this outside unloveliness is not faithfully reflected in the lives of the people ... Here, misery, filth and squalor

The backstreets of industrial towns were often fetid slums.

reign supreme. In his quest for ancient churches it has been the duty of the writer to explore these unpleasant districts with some diligence – certain it is that he does not desire to ever visit them again.

Joseph Morris, *The West Riding*, 1911

A century earlier, more British troops had been deployed to the textile manufacturing districts of the West Riding to suppress the Luddite rebellion than had been at Waterloo. Angry at attempts to introduce new processes that would force skilled men out of work and allow owners to employ women and children as cheap labour, the Luddites had turned to a campaign of sabotage and intimidation. They drew an armed response from the government that only ended once the area was brought under military control, and a series of show trials at York sentenced sixty men to harsh penalties ranging from execution to deportation and new laws made 'machine breaking' a capital offence.

The result of the military crackdown on workers was to create a deep mistrust of the military across the north, and especially of the part-time militia and yeomanry forces led by the local gentry. So when, in 1908, the various militia, yeomanry and volunteer forces were brought together into a single Territorial Force charged with home defence duties in case of invasion, the Trades Union Congress declared membership of the Territorial Force to be incompatible with trade union membership,

As they are thereby liable to be called out in times of industrial dispute to quell, and possibly shoot down, their fellow workers who are struggling to better their conditions.

James O'Grady, Independent Labour Party MP for Leeds East

Melodramatic as O'Grady's comment may seem today, at the time the prospect appeared all too real. The rapid expansion of towns created slums where poverty and disease were rife. In the industrial areas, the summer of 1899 saw one in four babies die before their first birthday, mainly of preventable diseases like diarrhoea caused by flies swarming into nearby houses from stinking, overflowing privies where one toilet could be shared by twenty households. The Boer War of 1899–1902 meant a need for extra troops for the British Army. Although plenty of volunteers came forward, the government was concerned to find that so many would-be recruits failed even the most basic medical examinations due to ill-health directly linked to the effects of poverty. After decades of poor housing, long working hours, poverty and malnutrition, people had had enough.

Child workers sorting coal. Within living memory, children as young as five had worked underground in the mining industry.

In 1908, more days were lost to industrial action than in the entire previous decade and in 1909, a series of strikes hit the coal industry. This led to Winston Churchill, Home Secretary, ordering troops into South Wales to restore peace among the 30,000 striking miners after Prime Minister Asquith made it clear that the government would use all its resources to enforce order. Plans to mobilise the Territorial Force were vetoed for fear that they might, as local men, side with the strikers. So began 'the great unrest'.

Between 1910 and 1914, the number of industrial disputes rocketed, reaching a peak of 872 in 1912 with forty million days lost to strikes – ten times the total of any previous year. As part of one national dispute, the seaman's strike in Hull saw 500 police officers drafted in from London to control the crowds after rioting began. Matters came to a head in Liverpool on 13 August 1911 when a crowd of 80,000 people marched to the city's St George's Hall, where local police had been reinforced by officers from other areas and by troops of the Warwickshire Regiment.

Fighting broke out with 186 people were taken to hospital for treatment, and 96 others arrested, triggering two nights of rioting. More troops were drafted in supported by a naval gunboat moored in the Mersey, and the Riot Act was read out. On 15 August, prison vans transporting many of those arrested to court were escorted by armed cavalrymen of the 18th Hussars but were attacked by a crowd on Vauxhall Road. Bottles and bricks were hurled at the soldiers as rioters tried to grab the reins of their horses. Fearing for their lives, the Hussars opened fire, killing twenty-year-old John Sutcliffe and twenty-nine-year-old Michael Prendergast, and wounding three other men. Since the strikers included railwaymen, the government found it could not move troops around the country to respond to local flare ups as other areas protested the killings in Liverpool. Four days later, and ironically just as the strike was being settled, two more men were killed during more rioting in Llanelli when soldiers facing a hostile mob again opened fire. Across the country, up to 50,000 troops were eventually deployed to maintain order as strike after strike broke out. In Leeds, where armed troops had been deployed to guard the city's railway stations, a meeting was held to protest against the arrest of Thomas Mann for publishing a pamphlet urging soldiers not to obey orders to fire on protesters. The demonstrators were urged,

Don't don the King's uniform, don't take the King's shilling. Until you know that you will not be called upon to shoot your fellow working men, don't join the army.

Robert Escritt, Independent Labour Party MP
and City Councillor for East Leeds

Alongside the industrial unrest came other forms of social protest. The women's suffrage movement had found a strong following in Yorkshire, with a large contingent of women from the West Riding taking part in attempts to storm the House of Commons in 1907. An appeal had been made for women willing to risk arrest to publicise their cause:

Manningham Mills, Bradford. Like many workplaces, built to display the fortunes of the owners.

Let me go, Mother. I am quite capable. I understand what I am fighting for, and am prepared to go to prison for the cause. I feel that women ought to have their rights and it will be an honour to go to prison.

Dora Thewlis, aged seventeen, Huddersfield

Suffragists (male and female) supported the political campaign to grant the right to vote to women. Suffragettes, however, took their protests to another level. Over the coming years, extremists among the movement began a campaign of vandalism, arson and even bomb attacks, on prominent politicians and businessmen. Small explosive packages were used to blow up postboxes and a larger device was discovered at the pumping house of a reservoir near Penistone in May 1914. Not all women supported the struggle:

Will no-one protest in the name of our common womanhood against the conduct of our Suffragettes? That they have become a deadly peril to the national life has long been apparent, but when deputations of women, calling themselves non-militant, importune our King and Ministers with senseless petitions when the militants continue to endanger life and property, and when, as on Sunday last, they interrupt the solemn services of our churches, the women of England who deserve that noble title should rise in their millions and protest. I would venture to suggest that the Press should from henceforth ignore the Suffragettes in toto, neither publishing their letters nor describing their outrages.

Edith Milner, Letter to *Yorkshire Evening Press*

As the final year of peace came to a close, it was a time for reflection:

As we look back over 1913 we must all feel that it was a year marked by a spirit of unrest … Most of us, I feel sure, will not regret the dawning of 1914.

Revd P. D. Woods, *Royston Parish Magazine*

Unfortunately for Revd Woods and his parishioners, 1914 brought no respite. Most worryingly for a county with a large Irish population, both sides of the divide in Ireland were openly preparing for a civil war that many feared would spill over into armed revolt in towns and cities on the mainland too. In February 1914, bombs 'of an Irish Republican type' were planted at the Leeds Municipal Power Station and at Harewood Territorial Barracks, where police reinforcements were being housed during yet another large scale strike (this time of Corporation Workers) and the chief suspect was an Irishman seen nearby shouting anti-British slogans. Soon after, poorly worded orders were issued to troops in Ireland in case of the expected uprising to prevent military arms stores being seized. These read as orders to fight Unionist volunteers whose stated aim was the protection of British interests in Ireland and which were seen by many officers as linked closely to the Army's own purpose there. As a result, the government faced a possible large scale mutiny by the Curragh garrison that was only averted by the diplomatic leadership of a number of senior officers. In the summer of 1914, the 'Irish Question' loomed ever larger in every local newspaper editorial and against this background of industrial and political unrest at home, the assassination of an obscure Austrian Archduke in faraway Sarajevo meant little to most people in Yorkshire.

The Austrian government regarded this crime as part of an organised movement by Servia [sic]. It stirred feelings of horror, true; but Leeds people, like other inhabitants of Great Britain, felt no particular apprehension as to the ability of statesmanship to compose the differences that arose. For several weeks our public and private affairs proceeded as usual. We had our own troubles – unrest in the industrial world, grave disorders in Ireland – but even these did not divert attention from the ordinary routine of business and pleasure.

William Herbert Scott

On the day of the assassination, 400 Huddersfield engineers walked out at the start of yet another strike which occupied most of the local press that week. But as the repercussions of those fateful shots began to be felt across Europe, the implications at home could not be ignored:

Though British affairs are inevitably of the utmost concern to British people, it nevertheless cannot but be recognised that the threat of war between Austro–Hungary and Servia [sic] is a matter of infinitely greater and wider importance ... Germany is the natural friend of England, and events during the last few years have been tending to establish the right relations between the two countries. To have been compelled to fight her in the interests of France and – much worse still – in those of obscurantist and reactionary Russia, would be not only a present misfortune but a permanent source of weakness, since we should have had a watchful enemy, kept waking by the fires of hate, waiting for the first opportunity to get in a deadly blow.

Huddersfield Daily Examiner, 27 July 1914

With a thriving export market throughout Europe, war among customers was a worrying prospect:

True it is that a general Continental war would in the end injure the prosperity of this country by greatly impairing the purchasing power of many countries which are now very good customers for the products of our manufactories. This calculation ... loses some of its effect from the fact that the extra production which immediate demands from France and Germany in case of war between those countries would occasion in many classes of goods, would go far to counterbalance the loss already mentioned. In the first instance, therefore, Britain has no immediate concern in the strife which is taking place or might take place if Russia, Germany and France should be drawn into the struggle ... Therefore Britain may continue to work for peace without any suspicion of selfish or improperly interested motives.

Huddersfield Daily Examiner, 31 July 1914

If Britain was to be drawn into the war, some believed it should signal the start of revolution:

The war is no concern of the working class and their duty is to take every advantage of such lapses into insanity by the capitalist class.

The Worker, I August 1914

Most people tried to carry on as normal, but the bank holiday crowds in Scarborough were reported to be 15,000 down on the previous year, and the movement of troops could not be ignored.

When war seemed imminent there were many in this country, and not a few in Todmorden, who thought that we as a nation should keep clear of the conflict. The issue was felt to be somewhat remote. Britain seemed to have small concern in the murder of an Austrian Archduke in a far-off Serbian town; but very few people in those early days had realised the real ambitions and designs of Germany, or knew how carefully for many years she had been maturing her plans for another great war of conquest as soon as a pretext could be found. That pretext was found in the Sarajevo assassinations … On the I August, while the issue seemed still hanging in the balance, the streets of Todmorden were filled with the usual Saturday night crowds, and the European crisis was deemed hardly more important as a subject of discussion than Todmorden's prospects of winning the Lancashire League Cup or the proposed Sunday opening of the Free Library newsroom, subjects which were just then occupying public attention. Sunday morning's news was a little more disquieting, and the congregations at churches and chapels were exhorted to pray that England might be spared the awful calamity of war. In the evening the town was thrown into a fever of excitement by the issue of a special edition of the Sunday papers reporting – without foundation, as it turned out later – a Naval engagement in the North Sea. Many people waited till the last possible moment on Sunday night to try to gain more definite information. None came, and morning brought no confirmation of the rumour, but made public the disquieting news that Germany had sent ultimatums to Russia and France … The first official communication received in Todmorden calling for definite action in connection with the threatened outburst, was a telegram received on Sunday afternoon, the 2 August, by Mr Thompson, the local station master, to the following effect: – 'Naval Reserves mobilised. Honour warrants, and give every facility for transit.' On the following morning Mr Taylor, the local postmaster, received instructions that the post office was to remain open all night until further notice for telegraphic business. Monday evening's papers, with reports of

Sir Edward Grey's speech in Parliament, provided official news of England's attitude in relation to the crisis, and the opinion was freely expressed that our hope of remaining neutral was now practically at an end. The streets were crowded with excited groups, discussing the situation, especially its possible effect on the nation's trade two or three mills had already taken the precaution of closing down for the Monday, and some for the Tuesday as well.

John A. Lee, *Todmorden and the Great War*

War is murder. It is the reign of hell on Earth. Workers, will you allow it? ... It is our immediate duty to make practical protest against this act of criminal folly – the European war.

Sheffield Independent, 3 August 1914

There is little poetry in present day war. Despite the mischievous efforts of one or two newspapers, the one question has been, 'Can we keep out of it with honour?'

Thomas Cox Meech, *Sheffield Independent*, 3 August 1914

Matters were rapidly spiralling beyond any diplomatic solution. On 1 August the British government ordered the mobilisation of the Royal Navy in response to the German government's general mobilisation of its forces and its declaration of war on Russia. In accordance with their treaty with the Russians, the French government also ordered general mobilisation, and the next day the German government sent an ultimatum to Belgium demanding passage through Belgian territory as part of their plan to outflank the main French defences along the Franco-German border. In effect, the Belgians were told to allow the free passage of German troops, in which case they would be allowed to remain a sovereign country or, if not, that they would be occupied as an enemy. To justify their threat, the Germans claimed that France was about to attack through Belgium and that French officers were already in the country, making their invasion an act of self-defence. In response to the threat, the Belgian king took immediate command of the army and prepared to fight:

The treaties of 1839, confirmed by the treaties of 1870 vouch for the independence and neutrality of Belgium under the guarantee of the [European] Powers, and notably of the Government of His Majesty the King of Prussia. Belgium has always been faithful to her international obligations, she has carried out her duties in a spirit of loyal impartiality, and she has left nothing undone to maintain and enforce respect for her neutrality. The attack upon her independence with which the German Government threaten her constitutes a flagrant violation of international law. No strategic interest justifies such a violation of law. The Belgian Government, if they were to accept the proposals submitted to them, would sacrifice the honour of the nation and betray their duty towards Europe.

Note delivered by the Belgian Minister for Foreign Affairs,
M. Davignon, to the German Minister in Brussels,
Herr von Below Saleske, 3 August 1914

German troops parade through Berlin on their way to the front, 1914.

With so many overseas territories, the British government could not ignore the threat to its own empire of allowing Germany to breach international law with impunity, nor could it allow the world's second most powerful navy to establish bases along the Channel coast. On 4 August, German troops crossed the Belgian border – an act even the German Chancellor admitted in a speech to the Reichstag was illegal:

Gentlemen, we are now in a state of necessity, and necessity knows no law! Our troops have occupied Luxemburg and perhaps are already on Belgium soil. Gentlemen, this is contrary to the dictates of international law. The wrong – I speak openly – that we are committing we will endeavour to make good as soon as our military goal has been reached. Anybody who is threatened, as we are threatened, and is fighting for his highest possessions can have only one thought – how he is to hack his way through.

Chancellor Bethmann Hollweg

My memories are those of a child, of course. I was in a small German garrison town in 1914 and I remember very well the tremendous enthusiasm. Of course, we schoolboys were all indoctrinated with great patriotism when war broke out. My father was an active infantry officer and I shall never forget the day when they marched out to the trains. All the soldiers were decorated with flowers, there was no gun which did not show a flower. Even the horses I think were decorated. And of course all the people followed them. Bands playing, flags flying, a terrific sort of overwhelming conviction that Germany now would go into war and win it very quickly.

Heinrich Beutow, German schoolboy

Britain was now faced with a choice. It could either honour its long-standing commitment to guarantee Belgian neutrality, or it could try to remain neutral and ignore a major European war on its doorstep. This would mean accepting the risk that once Germany had defeated the French and moved its fleet into ports along the English Channel it would then turn its attention to an England left without allies to support it. With Germany having demonstrated its willingness to flout international law, the risk was too great. Britain issued a demand that German troops be withdrawn from neutral Belgium by midnight on 4 August. In London as the deadline for a response approached, one *Times* correspondent found,

Two rival demonstrations in progress under Nelson's Pillar – on one side of the plinth for war, and on the other against! The rival crowds glared at

Crowds await news of the war, August 1914.

each other. Cries of 'The war does not concern us; we must keep out of it' were answered with cries of 'Down with Germany: the violator of Belgium'. I looked up at the effigy of Nelson – 'sailing the sky with one arm and one eye' – to see whether in imagination I could notice any change in his attitude. But no! He was still gazing steadily in a south easterly direction – towards France, the enemy – as he had been placed on his pillar eighty years ago ... At the approach of the decisive hour of eleven (midnight German time) when the ultimatum was to expire, we returned in our thousands to Whitehall ... Then followed the slow and measured strokes of Big Ben proclaiming to London that it was eleven o'clock. We listened in silence ... No-one came out of 10, Downing Street. No statement was made. There was no public proclamation that we were at war by a herald to the sound of trumpets and the beating of drums. The great crowd rapidly dispersed in all directions, most of them running to get home quickly and as they ran they cried aloud, rather hysterically, 'War!' 'War!' 'War!'

Michael Macdonagh

2

1914:
THE GREAT ADVENTURE

In the afternoon of my day on duty as Battalion Orderly Corporal, 4 August 1914, almost the whole of the regiment was free to wander off into Scarborough and enjoy the manifold entertainments. I was reclining near Battalion Headquarters when I heard the thud of a motor bike and as it approached I could see the dispatch rider was from the Corps of Signals. After dismounting, he carried a dispatch case into the orderly room. Within the space of a few minutes there was a sudden burst of excitement and a tense atmosphere prevailed. The voice of the RSM [Regimental Sergeant Major] boomed out, 'Bugler, sound Orderly Sergeants at the double'. From the prevailing peace of a quiet, hot sunny afternoon the whole scene was transformed into hectic activity. It was clear the dispatch contained orders of vital importance as the Adjutant gave orders for immediate striking of camp and plans were put out to collect the hundreds of troops enjoying their relaxation in the widespread coastal resort of Scarborough.

Lance Corporal A. G. Wilson, 5th West Yorkshire Regiment

News that war had been declared left communities across the country stunned as they awoke to the first day of the war.

At noon [on 4 August] a contingent of East Yorkshires marched into Kilnsea. At three o'clock three batteries of Field Artillery galloped into Kilnsea. As if this were not enough excitement at midnight a company of Northumberlands marched in. Kilnsea was a garrison town in under twelve hours. Great changes took place the next day. Soldiers were marched around the village to find them billets. Any place that was vacant was requisitioned. The Bluebell Cottage, then Cliff Farm which had been empty. Five hundred men made it their home for four months. The remainder of the troops were billeted in Easington, including the school building which meant no school for four months … for four months soldiers manned the trenches and were on duty twenty-four hours a day.

Ernie Norwood, eight-year-old schoolboy in Kilnsea when war
was declared

The immediate recall of the Territorials from their annual summer camps seemed to reinforce the fear of imminent invasion. As the 'Terriers' broke camp, they were given a few words of encouragement:

I am positively sure, I am positively sure that if the Germans land on our shores you will give them such a warm reception that they will never come again.

Earl of Harewood, Chairman of the
West Riding Territorial Association

In the absence of any real information, rumours spread like wildfire of a fierce naval battle raging in the North Sea; of an imminent airborne attack by troops carried in fleets of Zeppelins; of a landing by seaborne forces along the East Coast. With reliable news almost non-existent, local newspapers did what they could to keep their readers up to date, and many posted bulletins in their office windows where large crowds gathered to be read the latest communiques.

Fuelled by invasion scares over the past decade, householders were not prepared to take chances and rushed to stock up on essentials. By the end of Wednesday 5 August, the Huddersfield Industrial Society had sold all its stocks of flour and was still filled with shoppers two hours after its normal closing time, a scene repeated in every town and city in Yorkshire. Fearful that customers might withdraw their savings in cash and cause a run on gold reserves, all banks immediately shut their doors.

By Thursday, flour prices had risen from 1*s* 11*d* to 2*s* 6*d* per stone and sugar had risen by 7*d* per pound – equivalent to an increase of £2. 5 per pound in 2014.

This rise fell most heavily on small and struggling retailers in poor districts, who could not afford to keep large stocks. As a result they had to increase prices for their customers, and the poorer classes were made to pay.

Sir John Hammerton

Reports began to circulate of food riots and looting. As the situation threatened to escalate, representatives of the large grocery firms and the Grocer's Federation were called to a meeting with the government to ensure maximum retail prices were set for certain essential foodstuffs and a supply of sugar was compulsorily purchased by the government for sale at a fixed price. Gradually, some sort of order was restored but, for the poorer families in particular, food would remain a problem for the rest of the war.

Meanwhile, many thousands of ex-servicemen remained liable to be recalled to the colours for duty as part of the Army or Naval Reserves. Recall notices had been sent out by post or delivered by local police officers but those types of jobs had frequently preferred to recruit ex-servicemen and so in many cases, postmen and policemen found themselves among the first recalled. As mobilisation continued, it began to impact on more and more aspects of everyday life. Postal services were repeatedly cut back as staff left for war, bus drivers and conductors disappeared and in Hull, audiences for the Three Aeros trapeze act were disappointed when the news broke that the trapeze artists, too, had been recalled to service. At the same time, the railways had been taken over for government service and motor vehicles, carts and horses were all at risk of being commandeered. Ships laden with export goods remained in ports until a decision could be made about the insurance risk posed by the powerful German navy. Signs appeared in mills and factories announcing short time working brought about by the problems of simply moving goods around and many workers found themselves suddenly laid off. In Halifax, the West Yorkshire Federation Emergency Committee of Homing Societies met at the Saddle Hotel and decided, in view of the international crisis, to end the pigeon racing season early.

By Friday 7 August, some semblance of normality was returning to the country. Banks reopened so that wages could be paid but with instructions that staff could refuse to allow customers to make large withdrawals without good reason. To preserve gold reserves, bank notes were issued but needed some explaining:

Yesterday the Halifax banks reopened and there was nothing in the nature of a panic ...The issue by the government of the £1 and 10 [shilling] notes will be a big relief to the gold. The notes were issued in London yesterday and some were received by the Yorkshire Penny Bank from their head offices in London ... The alteration from coins to paper money will make no difference. The notes will be offered and accepted in payment just the same as gold and should be treated by the public with the same confidence. Wages paid in paper will have exactly the same purchasing power as if paid in gold and workers need have no hesitation in accepting them... The new £1 notes are printed on small slips of paper 2½ in by 5 in. They bear the following wording printed in Old English type:

'These notes are a legal tender for a payment of any amount. Issued by the Lords Commissioners of His Majesty's Treasury under authority of Act of Parliament

ONE POUND

(Sd) John Bradbury

Secretary to the Treasury'

On the left hand side they bear the King's portrait amid ornamentation encircled by the inscription 'Georgius V DG Britt Om Rex FD Ind Imp'. The notes are printed on white paper, watermarked with the royal cipher.

Halifax Courier, 8 August 1914

At the end of the first week of war, as the initial reaction wore off, people had time to reflect on what had happened. True, bank holiday tourists in London had been in a celebratory mood at the announcement of war – coming as it did after a day in the pub – but news of war was far from universally welcomed:

London is back in the mafficking* mood, and the blood lust has gripped its people. I hope the provincial towns are meeting the crisis in a far more serious mood. I wish I could blot from my memory the scenes of the last three days. They have been of the kind that shakes one's faith in all those things that make for moral and spiritual advancement in mankind ... I confess I was appalled at the light hearted wrecklessness [*sic*] of my fellow men and women. Judging by the demonstrations of the crowd it might have been a picnic the nation was entering upon instead of the greatest crisis of a century – shouting, singing, cheering mobs; besides themselves with blood lust and war intoxication. They shouted patriotic songs, sang 'Rule Britannia' they clamoured on the tops of the buses, waved miniature Union Jacks and generally conducted themselves in a way that proved they could have no idea of the gravity of the situation. I cannot blame them too much, however, for inside the House of Commons there was a recklessness and enthusiasm for the war that was horrible to witness ... I feel sure my constituents will understand my position. I hate and loathe war; I believe we might have been kept out of it ... The days that are coming will try men's souls. I beg of all my fellow townsmen to do their best to meet the sorrow and suffering that is bound to come...

[*Mafeking was a British garrison town besieged during the Boer War. Its relief had sparked widespread patriotic celebrations and given rise to a new word 'Mafficking']

James Parker MP, *Halifax Courier*, 8 August 1914

Mr Parker was not a lone voice. As the last hours of peace ticked away, a meeting called by the vicar for the inhabitants of New Mill agreed a resolution:

'That this meeting of inhabitants of the Holmfirth Division of New Mill and district urges the Government to maintain Britain's neutrality in the present crisis unless her interests are clearly and plainly attacked'. The unique character of the meeting lay in the fact that it appeared to comprise the entire population of the village. All parties took part in its promotion, and both men and women of all ages attended and followed the proceedings with a significantly silent but keen interest. As one of the speakers remarked, whatever might be the news of the following day as to the declaration of war, the people of New Mill would always have the satisfaction of knowing they had publicly expressed their convictions in favour of peace.

Huddersfield Daily Examiner, 6 August 1914

By that first weekend, patriotic fervour had already begun to claim victims. The *Halifax Courier* of 8 August reported,

Colonel Alfred Tufnell Robson, who hanged himself at his home in Gorleston, left a letter to the Coroner, which was read at the inquest last night. It contained the following; 'The strain of this terrible crisis is too much for me. I feel I am too old in my seventieth year to do anything for my country and only make an additional mouth to feed. Therefore I had better go at once'. The deceased had commanded the Gordon Highlanders in India.

That same day, a new piece of legislation passed almost unnoticed. It began as a simple paragraph published in the *London Gazette*:

(1) His Majesty in Council has power during the continuance of the present war to issue regulations as to the powers and duties of the Admiralty and Army Council, and of the members of His Majesty's forces, and other persons acting in His behalf, for securing the public safety and the defence of the realm; and may, by such regulations, authorise the trial by courts martial and punishment of persons contravening any of the provisions of such regulations designed –

(a) To prevent persons communicating with the enemy or obtaining information for that purpose or any purpose calculated to jeopardise the success of the operations of any of His Majesty's forces or to assist the enemy;

(b) To secure the safety of any means of communication, or of railways, docks or harbours; in like manner as if such persons were subject to military law and had on active service committed an offence under section 5 of the Army Act;

(2) This Act may be cited as the Defence of the Realm Act, 1914.

London Gazette, 8 August 1914

The Defence of the Realm Act (or DORA as it was generally known) was to govern the lives of every man, woman and child in the country for the next four years, granting draconian powers to control virtually all aspects of daily life. As one editor explained,

Under the Defence of the Realm Act (DORA), security was heightened around the country.

In other words, the military authorities could arrest any persons they pleased and, after court martial, inflict any sentence on them short of death. In addition, the military authorities were allowed to demand the whole or part of the output of any factory or workshop they required. They were also allowed to take any land they needed. This, in effect, made the civil administration of the country entirely subservient to the military administration.

Sir John Hammerton

By 1918, DORA would make it a criminal offence to speak in a foreign language on the telephone; to use invisible ink in a letter to another country (a common business tactic); to pass on a venereal disease to a serviceman; to fly a kite or whistle for a taxi (both of which were considered capable of acting as a signal to German bombers) or even to give a slice of bread to a dog (because of food shortages). Most annoying of all, many thought, DORA also governed where, when and with whom a man could drink. Concerns about alcoholism had been growing for years. In Britain, the Chancellor of the Exchequer, David Lloyd George, had led the campaign against what he saw as a national dependence on alcohol, claiming that Britain was 'fighting Germans, Austrians and Drink, and as far as I can see the greatest of these foes is Drink'. DORA immediately allowed for restrictions to be put in place to curb drinking by placing all pubs near naval dockyards and arms factories under the control of the military commander of the area. Getting a soldier or sailor drunk became a criminal offence and the buying of rounds was first discouraged and, in time, made illegal. Later amendments to DORA reduced drinking hours in all pubs from the pre-war 5 a.m. until 12.00 a.m. allowing them to open for alcohol sales just twice a day at 12.00 noon to 2.00 p.m. and 6.00 to 9.00 p.m. Such interference did not go down well with working men:

Hoyle's, the local soft drinks people, made a killing with 'Hop Ale'. It looked like bitter beer – in colour only! – And there was another drink called 'After Nine Stout' which was a form of dandelion and burdock. There was also a horrible concoction called 'Vegale', a hot soupy drink that smelt to heaven of peas. Nobody bought it. We were also allowed to sell Bovril and Oxo but they weren't very popular with the men at the bar.

Eva Leach, King's Head, Keighley

DORA was intended, amongst other things, to prevent the enemy gaining useful information, but its effect was also to even further restrict the flow of the little news that was available. As a result, people began to invent their own versions.

A very curious and persistent rumour has been circulated in Hull, coming from numerous very reliable people, none of whom, however, have it at first hand, that bodies of Russian troops have landed in Scotland for the purpose of proceeding to Belgium…

Hull Daily Mail, 30 August

The story quickly took on its own momentum around the entire country. Almost 200 trains full of Russians were said to have passed through York. A Scottish landowner boasted that 125,000 Cossacks had crossed his land. The *Daily Mail* quoted a reliable source, who claimed a million Russians had travelled through Stroud in a single night.

Friday 28 August: Report current in Braintree – that a Russian force has been brought to Yorkshire and landed there: and that the East Coast trains have been commandeered to transport them rapidly south en route for the French theatre of war…

Monday 7 September: Montague Edwards Hughes-Hughes, JP, of Leez Priory told me that an old servant of his had written that from her bedroom window she had watched train after train for hours, passing by night to Bristol. There were no lights in the carriages, but by the light of the cigars and cigarettes they were smoking, the black beards of the Russians could be seen…

Revd Andrew Clark

Revd Clark did not feel the need to question just how bright the cigarettes must have been for an elderly servant to be able to make out the smoker's beard on a darkened train at some distance, and in the middle of the night, but as the story grew, 'witnesses' told their audiences how the Russians, after days aboard ships from Archangel and long train journeys in the heat of an English summer, had boarded ships at the Channel ports with snow still on their boots. No matter how far-fetched the story might seem when the facts were examined, there were always at least a few people willing to believe it and pass it on. Finally, after weeks of speculation, the story was officially denied:

I am uncertain whether it will gratify or displease my honourable friend to learn that no Russian troops have been conveyed through Great Britain to the Western Front area of the European War.

Harold Tennant, Under Secretary of State for War, 18 November 1914

Although there were no Russians, there were thousands of others who found themselves in the wrong place at the wrong time. British tourists hurried back from the Continent with tales of their narrow escape from danger. Some found reaching home more difficult:

At the Barnsley West Riding Police Court on Friday two Roumanian peasants, man and wife, were charged on suspicion of stealing towels … the accused were found in possession of two or three towels bearing the name of the Cunard Steamship Company Ltd. They had tickets in their possession from Canada to Constanza (in Roumania) via Hamburgh but owing to the war they could not go through … they were seen on the Great Central Railway at Deepcar and arrested by railway officials who handed them over to the police … The police traced several addresses in the neighbourhood of Sheffield where they had applied for work but could not get any… Superintendent MacDonald said … true, they were aliens, but as far as his knowledge went they were friendly aliens.

Barnsley Chronicle, 19 August 1914

The lost couple were found work by the superintendent to tide them over, until a way could be found to get them home, but for such strays Britain was becoming an unwelcoming place. Suddenly, any foreigner was a potential enemy and a witch hunt got under way to uncover the spy rings everyone knew were hiding in every town, waiting for their chance to launch a campaign of murder and sabotage in preparation for the invasion, any unfamiliar face was immediately suspicious. A group of friends from Conisbrough were on a cycling holiday when war broke out and soon found themselves the focus of unwanted attention:

Very soon the spy scares began to sprout. People wondered who we were, wandering with a tent around the country, just as though a spy would carry around some distinctive mark. At one village in Worcestershire the local policeman came to identify us. The only mark of identity we could show was Harold's Post Office Savings Bank book. Things were getting so uncomfortable we decided to abandon our tour and make a beeline for home.

Bert Brocklesby, Conisbrough

Just as the stories of the Russians relied on the willingness of the audience to believe the story, so too spy stories often depended on the willing suspension of belief. An artist in the west of England found himself persecuted by rock-throwing youths and malicious complaints to the police on the grounds that he wore a wide brimmed hat. According to Caroline Playne, writing in 1931, the local schoolmistress explained the villagers' suspicions; 'If he is not a spy, why does he wear a hat like that?'

Soon, other stories began to spread.

A Rolls Royce of German registration was searched after its owners left for Germany and ... a large number of German and English maps were found in their car, together with detailed accounts of journeys made, a ruler, a whistle and a camera stand, some unused films and a quantity of rope. There were also a number of German newspapers with paragraphs marked in blue pencil relating to Irish Riots, insurrection in India, commercial war in England etc...

Yorkshire Observer, 15 August 1914

Many of the Germans still in London are unquestionably agents of the German government, however loose the tie may be ... They had in their possession arms, wireless telegraph apparatus, aeroplane equipment, motor-cars, carrier pigeons and other material that might be useful to the belligerent ... It has been remarked by the observant that German tradesmens' shops are frequently to be found in close proximity to vulnerable points in the chain of London's communications such as railway bridges ... The German barber seems to have little time for sabotage. He is chiefly engaged in removing the 'Kaiser' moustaches of his compatriots. They cannot, however, part with the evidences of their nationality altogether, for the tell-tale hair of the Teuton will show the world that new Smith is but old Schmidt writ small.

Editorial in *The Times*, 25 August 1914

If you saw somebody in the street that was a bit strange, somebody perhaps with a black beard, kids would run after them shouting 'you're a German spy'. Someone you hadn't seen near your terrace before, who just happened to be looking around, was automatically a German spy.

Florence Mower

The pigeon racers of Halifax had made a wise decision as they, too, fell under suspicion of communicating with the enemy. Soon, almost any pretext was enough. Louis Alexander Mountbatten, Marquess of Milford Haven, had been born as Prince Louis Alexander of Battenberg. After enlisting in the Royal Navy at the age of fourteen, and serving loyally for forty years, he had risen to the rank of First Sea Lord in 1912 but found himself hounded out of office in

October 1914 by unfounded press claims. Elsewhere, Lord Haldane, the Lord Chancellor and the man responsible for the reforms that had made the British Army ready for war found himself accused of being the Kaiser's illegitimate brother and of fraternising with Germans, to such a degree that his maid was required to burn hate-mail by the sack. Dachshunds were attacked in the streets and even killed, although fewer patriots appear to have been prepared to attack German Shepherd dogs, quickly renamed 'Alsatians' to link them to the French province (a change that would remain in place until 1977 when the Kennel Club reverted to the original name).

In Bradford, a large German population had integrated into the community to such a degree that many civic figures came from German families and employed thousands of local people in a trade almost entirely dependent on export sales to Germany. Streets in the city bore the names of German cities and regular church services were celebrated in German. The local Chamber of Commerce had been created in 1851 with two German Jews, Jacob Unna and Jacob Behrens, as founder members, and in 1863, Charles Semon, a native of Danzig, was made mayor. He was followed in 1910 by Jacob Moser, an industrialist and philanthropist from Kappeln in Schleswig Holstein, who became Lord Mayor of Bradford and its Chief Magistrate. With such strong links, the local reaction to Britain's enemy was perhaps more sympathetic than most:

It is a matter for much congratulation that so far there have not been in this country any popular demonstrations. Their position [Bradford's German population] is indeed terribly distressing and it would be a brutal and disgraceful thing to add to the misery which war must inevitably cause them by any demonstration.

Yorkshire Observer, 15 August 1914

The same was not true of other towns. Shortly after 9 p.m. on the night of 29 August, a drunken man by the name of Kelly walked into a butcher's shop owned by a naturalised German family named Andrassy on Church Green, Keighley, to buy Polony sausage. Rising costs were a major issue by that time and an argument about the price of the sausage led to Kelly being thrown out, later claiming to have been assaulted by the shopkeeper. He returned soon afterwards with a group of friends and attacked the shop, smashing its windows. As a full scale riot threatened to break out, Father Joseph Francis Russell from St Anne's Catholic church hurried into town and helped calm

The Evening Post

MONDAY, AUGUST 31, 1914.

KEIGHLEY HAS A STORMY WEEK-END.

GERMAN SHOPS ATTACKED.

POLICE DRIVE BACK RIOTERS WITH THEIR BATONS.

Wild scenes have occurred in Keighley over the week-end, culminating in a pitched battle between the police and the crowd, in which the latter came off second best.

Ever since the arrest of several Germans in Keighley feeling has increased against persons of their

Report on the Keighley riots.

the situation as the police responded quickly, dispersing the mob and taking the Andrassy family and their servants to the police station for safety. But this was only the beginning.

Anticipating further trouble the next day, local police drafted in seventy reinforcements from surrounding towns. Shortly after 10 p.m. on the Sunday night, a 'dense crowd' of up to a thousand people was reported to be gathering in the town centre. Soon the mob again attacked Andrassy's shop in what the *Yorkshire Post* would describe the following day as 'an organised raid' and set it on fire before turning their anger on other pork butchers in the town, including those owned by the Hoffman and Schultz families – despite both families also being naturalised British citizens. The shops were looted, as were nearby shops totally unconnected with the original targets, including a bootmakers and an unsuccessful attempt to loot a jewellers. With a recent strike still causing resentment, the mob then turned its attention away from Germans and towards Sir Prince Smith, one of the town's largest employers, who had been holding out against the strikers' demands. Leaving the town centre behind, the crowd marched towards his home on Spring Gardens Lane but as they approached the property, mounted and foot police hidden in the grounds charged the crowd and 'used their batons freely. Many people suffered'. The crowd fell back towards the town centre, rocks and bottles were hurled at the police. Another butcher's shop was looted and windows in the police station and forty panes of glass smashed at the home of Police Superintendent Birkhead. At around midnight, the police used their batons to clear the street and by 1 a.m. the riot was over.

Because of the newspaper stories and gossip that went around, I'm afraid we disliked the Germans very much. There were dreadful stories of the atrocities in Belgium, babies being bayoneted and women treated unspeakably. There were several small pork butchers in Keighley. Some of them had been there for generations, but they all had German names – there was Stein and Schultz and Schneider and Hoffman – and all these shops were attacked and looted … It was a Saturday night and we children were playing in the upstairs sitting room while our parents were busy at the bar … Near the pub was an Irish club. It was usually pretty noisy on Saturdays, so on the night of the riot we kids didn't take much notice of all the noise. Then my father came upstairs and he said, 'I want you children to see this. You'll never forget it!' We scurried into our clothes and went out with my father (my mother didn't approve so she stayed behind) … The was a great crowd there, mostly Irish from the Turkey Street district which was a poor quarter, and they were mostly drunk … The Schulz family were a nice couple with a baby. They lived next door to friends of ours in Low Street and they were all very good neighbours. When the looters started attacking their shop, the Schulzes rushed next door and sheltered with the Mitchells until the trouble died down. Mrs Schulz was in an awful state, quite terrified … Of course we were sorry for them, but we children thought that it was quite natural. After all, they were Germans!

Eva Leach, Keighley

On Monday, the task of clearing up began. Looters appeared in court after police found sides of ham and bacon stored in cellars.

Arthur Little, a weaver who had previously served in the army, was given a week to re-enlist after being found guilty of being drunk and disorderly. Herbert Towers told how he saw others stealing from the shops and decided he should join in and was remanded to prison for stealing nine shillings' worth of bacon. The mayor expressed his understanding of public anger over the atrocity reports but condemned as 'cowardly and un-English' the attacks on 'unfortunate Germans who found themselves in England'. With mills closed on the Monday, sightseers came into town to witness the damage for themselves, some taking fragments of shattered glass as souvenirs. The police put on a show of force with 148 men including eight mounted policemen in town and with a further twenty-five officers stood by in Bradford in case of any further violence and forces in nearby towns were alerted. For the authorities, the riots were hard to define – certainly anti-German sentiment had played a part but the attack on Sir Prince Smith's home showed that the true causes were much harder to pin down.

Similar scenes were reported from around the country:

There were a public outcry against all the Germans. Anybody that had a pork butchers shop with a German name, their windows were going in regular, and there was a lot of pork butchers in Bradford at that period. Where I lived in Manchester Road there were the Stieges, the Susslers – two Susslers – and the Lamonts, and they all set about them, it were all propaganda. It was just … well it was an outcry against the Germans.

John McGrath, 2nd Bradford Pals

As spy mania escalated, attention turned to German owned properties and their value as military positions.

Is it too much to ask that our kid gloved government will ascertain how many German owned factories have been built in this country which incidentally command Woolwich, Dover, Rosyth? A timely inspection might reveal many concrete structures.

Letter to *Daily Mail*, 3 October 1914

The idea of secret German installations ready to provide positions for heavy artillery quickly took root. Similar letters sprang up in local papers complaining of suspicious buildings built several years earlier or even of tennis courts laid near big houses that could serve as a platform for German guns. Few people seem to have considered that in order to install heavy guns on the pre-prepared concrete bases the Germans would need to have already taken control of the area or that in the meantime they might happily make use of British owned factories with concrete floors from which to fire their weapons.

To the Editor of the *Barnsley Chronicle*
Sir,
Since reading of the police raids at Willesden and Edinburgh, resulting in the finding of German preparations for the mounting of guns I have wondered if there are any German foundations for guns waiting in Barnsley. While I lived in Barnsley some years ago there was a building erected in 'Pitfields' near the Queen's Grounds. There seemed a certain amount of mystery about the place. The site was well boarded round before building work commenced and it was rumoured that a German firm was erecting a factory there. I know that the foundation and floor were substantial as I saw them laid, of course, without asking permission. So far as I am aware, the place has never been used as a works or a factory since being built. Of course it may have been used and might be quite all right in every way, but unless it is British owned, I think that if I were a Barnsley police officer I should be having a look round there.

'Old Barnsleyitte', Brighouse, 20 October 1914

Most significant of all, the sheer numbers of Germans became a political issue:

I do not move my Amendment with any hostility to the Germans in our midst. For many years England has been the home of foreigners, but I think they should be the first to realise that our first duty is to protect ourselves, and I would rather that irreparable damage should be done to any individual or individuals rather than our country should be placed in danger even for a moment. There are a very large number of aliens registered in this country at the present time. On the 9 September the Home Secretary gave us some figures, and he told us that there were 50,633 alien Germans registered in this country, and 16,014 Austrians. If we were to add ten per cent for non-registration up to that date, then we should get a total of over 73,000 alien enemies. I know it is a very difficult matter to say that A or B is a spy, nor could the Germans or the French say that A or B was a spy before they found him out. I think we are entitled to consider here what happened in the case of France and Belgium. There they have found a complete system of espionage. Soldiers, sailors, policemen, telephonists, tram drivers, professional men of every kind, and men of every class in the working life of France and Belgium have turned out to be spies. Any officer or soldier who has returned from the front will tell you that those countries have been infested with spies. Now England is a greater enemy to Germany than either France or Belgium. The enmity of Germany is more directed against us at the present time and has been for some years past, than against Belgium or France ... On the other hand, England has been the easiest country to enter, and therefore it is fair to assume that as we are considered the greatest enemy of Germany and as ours is the easiest country to enter, we have a larger number of spies than either Belgium or France. You may say that this does not matter unless Germany invades us, but we must prepare for eventualities. Personally, I am not one of those who think that we shall be invaded, but we must prepare for eventualities. If there is no possibility of invasion, why is the Government providing against it? Why are trenches, wire entanglements and other reasonable precautions which sane men would take to protect us being prepared by our military advisers? I think those who are responsible for dealing with the spy question should take the same steps to protect the country against the possibility of trouble from spies as the military authorities are doing ... I have a return here, not of Germans who are registered to-day, but of Germans who were registered in the Census returns three years ago, and it shows a very small proportion of people registered then as Germans compared with the number of Germans we now find to be in the country. I think I am right in saying that in England and Wales alone there were only about 13,000 as given in the Census returns, whereas now we know that there are something like 56,000. Of that number an enormous proportion were in Kent, Sussex, Essex particularly, and Yorkshire – all those counties along the East Coast of England. Hon. Members may laugh, but why did those men go and settle there, unless it was with some intention of being useful to their own friends if and when the day came, possibly even of an invasion of Great Britain. The Home Secretary has always been an optimist. He dealt with this matter last Session in the most optimistic spirit. He told us that nobody had been shot.

Mr Joynson-Hicks MP, *House of Commons Reports*,
12 November 1914

Steps were already being taken to control 'the enemy within':

'Advice to Aliens now in Britain' was yesterday issued by the British Government as below:

German subjects must register themselves at the nearest police station. British women who have married Germans have become German citizens and must be registered. The children of such marriages are in a similar position. Foreigners desirous to leave will find no difficulty unless German subjects if they provide themselves with passports etc and make sure beforehand of train and boat services ... Permits are only given to leave Britain by certain ports on a given date by a given steamship service. Therefore applying to leave should make sure of being able to leave a day or two before.

Barnsley Chronicle, September 1914

As Reservists returned to their units and Territorial Force soldiers received their mobilisation papers, other local people were also being recalled:

During the weekend quite a number of young Germans residing in Bradford left the city in order to rejoin their regiments. Yesterday about thirty departed for London on the 2. 5 p.m. train. They were seen off by friends and the German pastor.

Yorkshire Observer, 5 August 1914

Under the orders of the Home Secretary, German and Austrian subjects living in Britain had been given until 10 August to leave and any German remaining after that date was required to register at the local police station by 17 August, Austrians by the 23rd, or face a possible £100 fine or six months imprisonment. Long queues of businessmen, nannies, students, tourists stranded by the war and old men and women who had left their homeland as children formed and stood patiently for hours before being processed.

The Bradford registration of aliens is now complete and shows a larger proportion of Germans and Austrians within our city than many people might imagine. Many of these occupy important positions in our commercial life and may be regarded as friendly. They will have no use of a telephone or motor car and all their correspondence is subject to careful scrutiny. They are not allowed to leave town without a police permit.

Bradford Daily Telegraph, 20 August 1914

Meanwhile, after the German reservists left Bradford, other young men with names like Muller, Hamlin, von Halle and Bernhardt were seen off from the same Bradford station on the 20 August by the Mayor and Chief Constable as they set out for officer training in the British Army. Norman Muller, from Cononley near Keighley would die leading his troops into battle in 1918 and was the son of Colonel George Herbert Muller, the first commander of the Bradford Pals and himself the son of a German immigrant. By the following July, the House of Commons heard that:

'Enemy aliens' being marched into captivity.

In looking through the list of the staff in the War Office, in the July Army List, you will find such names as these, serving the country: Schlich, Bovenschen, Dannreuther, Rueker Munich, Underlin, Varrelmann, Ackermann, Umlauf. If anyone will take the trouble to look amongst the list of officers in the Army List for July, he will find that there are 135 officers whose names begin with 'Sch'. There is no really British name, to my knowledge which begins with 'Sch'.

Sir Richard Cooper

However willing to serve their country some Britons of German descent might be, there were many more whose loyalty was in doubt. Police and army patrols were sent to round up German males deemed to present a threat to national security. It was not always clear what threat someone posed:

The pride of our heart, however, remained with us Billie. Billie was twenty-two, but looked eighteen and the most typical English boy one could find anywhere. Which is exactly what he was. He was just a jolly English schoolboy with an irresistible smile who quite saw the fun of the situation. He could not speak a word of any language but English, and as to Germany he hardly knew it existed. He had never seen a German before he came to [the camp], but he made friends with everyone and was adored by most, certainly by all the ninety per cent who – as everywhere throughout the war were bad 'haters'. Billie's parents had emigrated to Australia when he was quite a little boy, and they had died out there. He had studied architecture and was passing his summer holiday in Europe. When war broke out he was in Belgium and came to England at once – without a passport, for before the war hardly anyone ever troubled to take out a passport, and even less to take one with him when travelling. Billie landed in Southampton and thought some of the buildings of that port quite interesting. So he started sketching them, and was promptly arrested, for the interesting buildings happened to be part of the fortifications. He had no papers, so the authorities decided he could only be a German. I imagine that even they must have thought him and his sketching too naive for a spy, but a German he would remain until he could prove another nationality, and so there he was amongst his 'compatriots'. He hoped to get his papers from Australia very soon, he told me, he had already waited ten months for them, meanwhile he intended to remain cheerful and did not despair of organizing football in the camp. Billie was not only popular on account of his charming smile, but also as a living proof of the utter lack of sense of the British authorities – which everyone felt they had shown in his own case as well – and because his presence consoled people in a way, for what could you expect if even Billie had been locked up! – I have often wondered if his papers ever arrived or what became of him.

Paul Cohen-Portheim, German Internee

Temporarily held in police stations and army camps, these civilian internees were released back to their families if the local Chief Constable was satisfied they did not present a risk although they would not be allowed to use telephones, their correspondence was subject to censorship and they would require special permits to travel more than 5 miles from their homes. Those deemed a greater risk were sent to internment camps being set up around the country, including one of the most unusual prison camps established during the war – the Lofthouse Park Zivilinternierungslager at Wakefield.

Built by the Yorkshire West Riding Electric Tramway Company and opening at Whitsuntide 1908, Lofthouse Park was Britain's first amusement park. Created around a country house and its

Lofthouse Park Zivilinternierungslager (Civilian Internment Camp) Wakefield.

grounds, at the entrance was a decorative arch lit by coloured light bulbs and inside there was a pavillion with a theatre and a cinema screen, a bandstand and a helter skelter, a privet hedge maze, a hall of mirrors and a haunted house called 'Kelly's Cottage' along with a roller skating rink. The camp had three sub-divisions. First to be created was the south camp around the concert hall which contained a stage and an auditorium and soon become a rabbit warren full of beds, chairs, clothes, and men. As the camp filled, some wooden huts were added along with a hospital and barracks block. Later, a north camp was built using rows of long, low, wooden huts and there was a corrugated iron hall presented by an Anglo-German donor. Finally, a west camp of corrugated iron huts was built on was a treeless, grassless, waste ground adjoining the main camp. Each area was sealed and special permission was needed to move from one division to another. As a result, each developed its own character. Paul Cohen-Portheim, a German artist who spent much of the war at Lofthouse, recalled how the South Camp housed men who had dealings in African colonies and who were 'inclined to be cranky'. The North Camp was 'rigid and correct' and regarded themselves as socially superior. He himself lived in the West Camp, which,

Had the least character and was the most colourless and monotonous of the three. It was essentially middle-class. Nearly all its inmates were business men who had lived in England before the war; a very few in a big way of business, but mostly men of moderate means. There was a majority of middle-aged, a minority of young men, mostly city clerks.

Paul Cohen-Portheim

Lofthouse was considered to be a 'privilege' camp for which inmates had to pay ten shillings per week for the privilege of being held there but conditions were at least tolerable. A theatre group was established, men were able attend classes in various subjects (although German academic establishments later refused to recognise the courses as had been hoped). Men were given garden plots to tend, musical instruments were provided and even an art studio was available. But even such luxuries did not detract from the fact that the men were being held prisoner and forced to part from their families.

In Germany, a similar round-up had seen British men – some of them former German citizens – arrested and placed into similar camps. One such, at Ruhleben, held enough Yorkshiremen to ensure a good cricket team able to take on their Lancashire counterparts. Some were sailors in port when war broke out, some students, others businessmen and engineers representing their company's German interests.

The internment of German men created a problem. Under the terms of the 1870 Naturalisation Act, any British woman marrying a foreigner automatically lost her citizenship and, in the eyes of the government, took her husband's nationality, even if she was later widowed or separated. If a German born man took British citizenship, then his British-born wife could be issued with a certificate to confirm her new status – as a Briton. By November 1914, wives were also required to register and suddenly, hundreds of women and children who had been born and raised in Yorkshire found themselves aliens in their own homes.

An agreement had been reached that the British-born wives of internees would be given welfare payments by the German government via the American embassy for an amount similar to the separation allowances paid to the families of serving soldiers. In return, the British government would support the German-born wives and children of British men held in German internment. This arrangement might have worked well for Britain since there were far more Germans in Britain but Germany ended its payments in November 1914, leaving 'hun-wives' without any means of support. A system was set up to provide families in Britain with money via the local Board of Guardians, but the German government refused to provide for British-born wives, leaving them to rely entirely on local charities.

After the initial enthusiasm and patriotism came a wave of quietness because then the first death lists were published in the papers. And my mother – she was English – was suddenly surrounded by women of the regiment,

Camp store, Lofthouse Park.

Barrack hut, at the British civilian internment camp, Ruhleben.

the wives of the other officers of course, and most of them – because my father's regiment was one of the first to march over the border into Belgium – were widows. And even as a child, I must say, it gave me a great shock to see that most of the officers were dead and killed during the first weeks. A lot of the younger soldiers were dead and the whole feeling of enthusiasm faded away very quickly in my opinion. The world became grey after that.

Heinrich Beutow, German schoolboy

Between May 1915 and June 1916, around 10,000 people, including men over military age, women and children, were repatriated to Germany and a steady stream of British people returned to the UK via neutral Holland – Lofthouse Camp becoming involved in negotiations to repatriate one prisoner's pet Dachshund. As animals were not allowed aboard Red Cross ships, diplomatic channels were opened to find a place on a neutral ship for the dog, which eventually was reunited with its owner.

Hull man David Russell, a black Jamaican and a British subject, was interned at Ruhleben and heard that his German-born wife – who spoke no English – and four children had been forced out of Leipzig and sent to England in January 1915. There was no policy of forced repatriation for women who had changed their nationality purely through marriage in either country and it seems likely that Russell's colour had a lot to do with the decision. Although technically British, Mrs Russell spoke no English. She and her children were German by birth and therefore the enemy. Their reception was likely to be at best indifferent and there was always the fear that their new neighbours might turn against them. It would be nine months before he learned the fate of his family. Within a week of their arrival, the destitute family had been forced into a Hull workhouse. Worse, the children, aged nine, six, two and one, had been forcibly removed from their mother in line with workhouse policy.

It is not practicable to arrange that a mother and children shall live absolutely as a family in a poor law institution. Hull Guardians have been instructed to allow Mrs Russell to see her children at reasonable intervals.

Letter to David Russell from Hull Guardians, September 1915

Meanwhile, other families were splitting up as their menfolk left for war. The first reservists rejoined their regiments immediately and within days were on their way to France. Their departure was closely followed by that of the Territorials as they left for training camps. Crowds turned out to cheer the men off and in some places schools closed so that children could wave their fathers goodbye.

The departure of the Leeds Rifles for Strensall Camp near York of 10 August

was witnessed by large crowds, and as the men marched through the centre of the city they were greeted with hearty cheers at many points. The men themselves seemed in very high spirits, and they responded enthusiastically to the good wishes shouted to them. There were a number of pleasing incidents on the way. As one of the lieutenants was leaving the barracks a catholic girl went up to him, and taking off her rosary she handed it to him with the remark 'Wear these. They'll bring you good luck.' The officer, who was greatly touched by the girl's sincerity, accepted the beads and slipped them on his neck underneath his tunic.

Leeds Mercury, 11 August 1914

The 'hearty cheers' of the newspaper version were remembered slightly differently by those who heard them:

Along York Road everybody came out to cheer us because they thought we were off to the front and those dreadful women all shouted – 'encouraging remarks' I'd better call them because I can't repeat them!

Bandsman John Sanderson,
8th West Yorkshire Regiment (Leeds Rifles)

The departure was marred by the death of thirty-seven-year-old Tom Beckwith, a Territorial with fourteen years' experience who was thrown from a recently commandeered horse that had become frightened by the noise and the crowd. Even this, though, did little to dampen the carnival atmosphere. Across the county, crowds turned out to see the local lads off and the sudden absence of so many young men around town was hard to ignore:

I had no idea there were so many, in some houses at which I called two or three of the family, husbands and brothers, drawn out were by no means uncommon. These are men drawn out to fulfill Garrison duty.

G. Thorpe, Hull

As the Reservists arrived in France and the Territorials mobilised, newly appointed Secretary of State for War Lord Herbert Kitchener quickly

Todmorden Territorials march away to war. Similar scenes were taking place across the county.

reached the conclusion that the war would be likely to drag on for at least three years, and would be costly in terms of casualties.

At least no-one can say that my colleagues in the cabinet are not courageous, they have no army and they declared war against the mightiest military nation on earth.

Lord Kitchener

The small professional army could not be expected to survive long against the overwhelming German forces pushing into Belgium and he began making plans for a massive expansion from six to a possible seventy divisions. Recruitment began immediately. Unfortunately, joining the Army was not an attractive prospect for young men brought up to regard it with suspicion.

The Duke of Wellington had famously referred to the British soldier as 'the scum of the earth' and even at the outbreak of war troops were routinely barred from music halls, theatres and pubs. 'Going for a soldier' was not something respectable young men should ever do. William 'Wully' Roberston left his post as a servant in the Earl of Cardigan's household to enlist underage in the 16th Lancers in November 1877. After twelve years as a trooper, 'Wully' began a meteoric rise which, by 1914, saw him as Quartermaster General for the British Expeditionary Force, and by 1916 he was Chief of the Imperial General Staff – Britain's highest ranking soldier – but he always remembered his horrified mother's first letter to him after he joined up:

You know you are the Great Hope of the Family … if you do not like Service you can do something else … there are plenty of things Steady Young Men can do when they can write and read as you can … I shall name it to no one for I am ashamed to think of it … I would rather bury you than see you in a red coat.

The outbreak of war changed attitudes towards soldiers but the problem of attracting recruits still remained.

Before mobilization, we were greatly below establishment. Leeds was a very unmilitary city, and we had to face a good deal of veiled hostility from various quarters: partly genuine pacifism – that is, opposition to war in any circumstances, partly an ancient prejudice connecting soldiers with immorality and drink, and partly, a strong objection felt by Trade Union leaders to their young members coming under the personal influence of the 'boss class' to which they conceived the officers to belong.

Major F. L. Watson, Leeds Rifles

Recruits came forward but they were not always what recruiters were hoping for:

Some men in D Coy refused to appear on group photographs in case copies should fall into the hands of the Leeds City Police.

Company Sergeant Major Joseph Carter,
7th West Yorkshire Regiment

Most of them were the biggest set of scruffs and roughnecks you ever saw in your life. Filthy dirty and like wild animals. We would never have dreamt of having fellows like them in the Volunteers. Some were sent to me and so was Grainger Rex whose father was a master builder in my home village - Garforth. He was a nice lad who'd been well brought up. When the food came up from the cookhouse, these awful roughs from the Bank went mad and grabbed the

Your King and Country Need You.

A CALL TO ARMS.

An addition of 100,000 men to his Majesty's Regular Army is immediately necessary in the present grave National Emergency.

Lord Kitchener is confident that this appeal will be at once responded to by all those who have the safety of our Empire at heart.

TERMS OF SERVICE.

General Service for a period of 3 years or until the war is concluded.

Age of Enlistment between 19 and 30.

HOW TO JOIN.

Full information can be obtained at any Post Office in the Kingdom or at any Military depot.

GOD SAVE THE KING!

Recruiting advert from 1914.

food like cannibals and never left any for poor Grainger who had to buy all his meals in the YMCA. I'm afraid these lads were beyond my control, but the two Regular sergeants who'd come to our Company to train us put a stop to this behaviour.

Lance Corporal Albert Bowden, Leeds Rifles

Dodgy though some volunteers may have been, Kitchener's New Army soon reached its target of 100,000 men and recruiting for 'K2', the second 100,000, picked up after stories reached home of the retreat of the army from Mons and especially when lurid tales of German atrocities in Belgium began to circulate. Like the stories of the Russian troops, it seemed that the more outlandish the tale, the more it was likely to be repeated. Among the reports was that of a Scottish nurse from Dumfries, twenty-three-year-old Grace Hume, who, according to the story, had left home at the start of the war to work in a Belgian hospital. When German troops captured the hospital, they murdered and beheaded the wounded men and cut off Nurse Hume's right breast, leaving her to die. As the national papers took the story, it grew. A second nurse named Millard wrote of how Hume had shot a German who attacked her patients and was tortured as a result. For almost two weeks the story ran in several papers until the *Times* revealed that not only did Nurse Millard not exist, but that Grace Hume had never left the country and was, in fact, working in Huddersfield, the whole story having been made up by her seventeen-year-old sister. Nevertheless, outraged young men heard such stories and came forward to stop the barbaric 'Hun' before they reached Britain. Inspired by a combination of patriotism and a belief that the country was under threat of immediate attack, men joined up.

We had been brought up to believe that Britain was the best country in the world and we wanted to defend her. The history taught us at school showed that we were better than other people (didn't we always win the last war?) and now all the news was that Germany was the aggressor and we wanted to show the Germans what we could do.

Private George Morgan, 1st Bradford Pals

There was, though, still some reluctance on the part of many in the class-conscious Edwardian world to the idea of mixing with common soldiery:

Sir, Are we not patriotic in Hull? Whether we are or not, the fact remains that recruiting for the army, so far as Hull is concerned, is very poor. I cannot

Recruiting rally, Dewsbury.

think that the shocking response to Lord Kitchener's appeal is due to either indifference or to cowardice. There must be a reason why young men are holding back. A friend of mine, a few days ago, expressed his intention of enlisting, he now states he will not do so unless more of his own class volunteer. What my friend is suggesting is this: that instead of some of the larger employers of labour in Hull giving big donations of money they should use their influence to organize Corps of the middle class young men – clerks, tailors, drapers' assistants, grocers, assistants, warehousemen and artisans. Then we should see men living, sleeping and training in company of others of their own class. It is the idea of having to herd with all types of men now being enlisted that keeps our young athletes and men of good birth and training from joining the colours. At least that is the opinion I have gathered from conversation with likely candidates. I am, Sir, etc.

'Middle Class', Letter to the *Hull Daily Mail*, 26 August

General Sir Henry Rawlinson was thinking along similar lines and suggested that they might be more inclined to enlist if they knew that they were going to serve alongside their friends and work colleagues. He appealed to London stockbrokers to raise a battalion of men from workers in the City of London to set an example and within a week in late August 1,600 men enlisted in this 10th (Service) Battalion, Royal Fusiliers – the so-called 'Stockbrokers' Battalion'. A few days later, the Earl of Derby set out to raise a battalion of men from Liverpool. Within two days, 1,500 Liverpudlians had joined what Lord Derby told them 'should be a battalion of pals, a battalion in which friends from the same office will fight shoulder to shoulder for the honour of Britain and the credit of Liverpool'. Within the next few days, he had enough men for three more battalions. Encouraged by Lord Derby's spectacular success, Kitchener encouraged similar recruitment campaigns throughout the entire country. Soon, towns and cities were vying to outdo each other in forming their own local battalions. Until ready to be handed over to the War Office, the recruitment and administration costs of such units were funded by the local authority or even by wealthy individuals as 'Pals' battalions sprang into existence almost overnight.

Today has seen the commencement of recruiting for the middle-class clerks and professional men, or the 'black coated battalions' … it must not be thought there is a desire for class distinction but just as the docker will feel at home amongst his every-day mates, so the wielders of the pen and drawing pencil will be better as friends together.

Hull Daily Mail, 2 September 1914

The advantage of the system described is that it restricts admission to the battalion to the right sort of men. An exact definition of suitability for this purpose can hardly be obtained but the ideal to be aimed at is a congenial companionship and a community of interest and association, and the question of suitability in this respect will be in the discretion of employers who distribute the tickets or the responsible league representatives who will supervise the registration and form their own judgement upon each of the men who come forward ... [Those judgements will be used to direct a recruit to the appropriate company]:

A Company	Professional men and Bradford Trade Employers
B Company	Cashiers, foreign correspondents, higher Grade office workers
C Company	Clerks
D Company	Warehousemen
E Company	Master Tradesmen
F Company	Tradesmen's Assistants
G Company	'Pals', meaning friends who wish to stand together despite differences of civilian occupation
H Company	Miscellaneous

Yorks Observer, 5 September 1914

[The idea of a new battalion] seems to have taken firm root in the minds of the young commercial and professional men of the city, who appear only too anxious to get started. This, of course, cannot yet be done, as the official sanction of the War Office to form the battalion has not yet been received, though it is expected at any moment. Thus the registration is not enlistment proper but a means of raising the battalion first of all 'on paper' after which it can be converted into actual existence in a very short time.

Yorks Observer, 14 September 1914

In Leeds and Sheffield, the universities set about forming their own battalions from students and the professional classes:

On September 3 I went down to Leeds Town Hall to join the local branch – ie Leeds Pals – of the West Yorks Regiment ... The main hall of the Town Hall had about sixty young fellows arguing rather excitedly, but I and a fellow whom I had told my intention to and was joining me, went up to a table at the top of the room where two or three well dressed, prosperous looking gents were seated. I was asked what my father did for a living, much to my surprise, and I suggested I wanted to join and not my father. I said I was a clerk, but they insisted I should say what my father did. It was curiouser and curiouser, but eventually I said he was a farm worker. Very politely, very firmly, it was told to me that only professional men's sons, or whose fathers had businesses, could join for a day or two – it was exclusive. My friend promptly nudged me and said he was going about his job, he never did join up ... well my patriotism wasn't very deep, and Belgian atrocities didn't cut much ice, but I was fearfully sick of a humdrum life that led nowhere and promised nothing, so I went to another recruiting depot and was enlisted as a gunner in the [Royal Artillery].

Gunner E. Robinson, Yarnley, Leeds

The exclusive nature of the early Pals battalions angered many of those turned away:

They was all the nobs Battalion, the Commercials used to snob you a bit, they was all clerks and teachers.

Private Ernest Land, 2nd Hull Pals

When our lads enlist on their own without fuss or bribery, they have to go where and with whom they are sent ... May I suggest that when the Lord Mayor equips his Feather Bed Battalion that he be sure not to forget dressing gowns, slippers, eiderdowns, whiskeys and sodas, and, if he can manage it, to throw in a few billiard tables. I have no doubt the battalion will greatly distinguish itself.

'Hunslet' Letter, to the *Yorkshire Evening Post*, 8 September 1914

We publish this letter so that, if comment of the kind is being made in the city, it can be answered effectively. 'Hunslet' takes a mean and narrow-minded view of the battalion. It will be equipped exactly like all other battalions of Lord Kitchener's Army, and will serve alongside any other battalion, no matter how or where recruited, and under exactly the same conditions. If 'Hunslet' is qualified to enlist, doubtless he will prefer to serve alongside his friends. This is just what the young men in business prefer to do, and doing it, they will enjoy exactly the same privileges given to all other soldiers in Lord Kitchener's Army and none other. We have already said that the labourer who enlists gives more than some of the business young men, because he gives the whole of his capital, but that is no reason for deriding the public spirit of these young men. When the labourer and the junior partner find themselves in the field together (as they will do if they have any luck) we venture to say they will be best of friends, and find in each other qualities that they had, perhaps, little suspected.

Editorial, *Yorkshire Evening Post*, 8 September 1914

Some battalions were highly selective in the type of person they would recruit. Hull, through the efforts of Lord Nunburnholme and the East Riding Territorial Force Association, would eventually provide four battalions of the East Yorkshire Regiment: the 10th (Hull Commercials) Battalion drawn from the city's banking and office workers; the 11th (Hull Tradesmen); the 12th (Hull Sportsmen) and a miscellaneous group unable to join the existing battalions known simply as the 13th (Hull t'others). Others formed around sporting connections, school alumni and workplaces. The idea, according to one observer, was that such battalions should be 'as much a social club as a military unit'. The *esprit de corps* developed over generations that held regular battalions together in the heat of battle would come instead from a shared local background.

The idea was attractive. Groups of friends marched themselves to the recruiting offices to join up together. For many, enlisting offered a chance to escape from the boredom and daily grind of their working lives, for others it was a patriotic duty.

I was the only lad working in a saw mill and I were doing all t'work. I went to t'boss, I says 'Can't you give me some more money?' He says, 'You'll get your rise when your birthday comes'. I never said a word to anybody. I went straight down and enlisted … It were a gimmick were Pals. How can I explain? They wouldn't get them to join now like they did in them days. Britons never shall be slaves? We were all slaves in't olden days, working in't mills.

Private Ernest Brook, 2nd Bradford Pals

There were four or five of us all at the same time all of an age. One followed another. We thought it was perhaps a holiday out of the pit, a change of life. I was under age but I was accepted. Wilf Paxton was with me. We'd always been pals from being at school. He was with me when we all joined up together. There were four of us really near to each other. We'd do anything for each other. We stayed in the same platoon until the beginning of 1917. There was a fellow with us, they called him Martin, he was a big hefty lad. When he went to be examined they said they'd never had a better specimen in front of them but two or three days later his mother came and chased him round the Public Hall with her umbrella. She brayed him down the steps and he never came back again. He was twenty-ish. He got away with it. How he did it I don't know.

Private Harry Hall, 13th York and
Lancaster Regiment (Barnsley Pals)

When they started the Pals battalion I wanted to get in very much. My brother-in-law had joined and four cousins had already joined so of course

I wanted to join. Only I was only sixteen. I thought I wouldn't be big enough 'cos I wasn't what you might call big, well made or owt. Just a skinny bit of a lad … And 'course I went and joined the queue to join the Bradford Pals and they were very particular who they took because such a lot wanted to join. They were very choosy about it all … they passed you from one doctor to another, one doctor would do one thing and another another and the last one was chest measurement. I thought it would be the end of the world if I didn't pass. People were being failed for all sorts of reasons, if they hadn't sufficient teeth, for example; they were glad to get them later! When I came to have my chest measured I took a deep breath and puffed out my chest as far as I could and the doctor said 'You've just scraped through.' It was marvellous being accepted. When I went back home and told my mother she said I was a fool and she'd give me a good hiding: but I told her, 'I'm a man now and you can't hit a man.'

Private George Morgan, 1st Bradford Pals

I said to the boss, 'I want to join the Army, I want to be released from my job'. So he said to me, 'here in the steelworks you are doing just as much for your country just as much for the nation, as though you were in the Army'. Well, I couldn't see myself catching the 8.40 to Brightside every morning and leaving for home in the afternoon, doing all the little jobs in the evening, and all the time my pals were suffering – probably dying somewhere – they were serving their country. I couldn't see myself carrying on in that particular way, so I said, 'I'm awfully sorry but I have made up my mind, I must go'. And he saw that I was determined and he said, 'Well then, go to the wages office and they will pay you whatever is due to you. But we shall not save your job for you when you come back and we shall not pay you anything while you are away.'. I said, 'All right, I accept those conditions'. My mind was made up, the die was cast, and when I finally joined the Sheffield Battalion, as 256, Private F. B. Vaughan, Sheffield Battalion York and Lancasters – all at a bob a day – you know I was a very happy man. It was not just a sudden decision that I made to join the Army. My pals were going, chaps I had kicked about with in the street, kicking tin cans or a football, and chaps I knew very well in the city. And then if you looked in the newspapers we saw that Canadians were coming, Australians were coming, South Africans were coming – they were catching the first available boat to England to get there before the war was over. Then when you went to the pictures you'd be shown crowds of young men drilling in Hyde Park or crowding round the recruiting office, or it might be a band playing 'Tipperary'. The whole thing was exciting, and even in the pulpits – although it started rather shakily at first – they eventually decided to come down on the side of the angels and blessed our little mission. I don't know whether patriotism entered into it or not, possibly so. We were stirred, I know, by the atrocities, or the alleged atrocities, when the Germans invaded Belgium and France. The other great factor was that the womenfolk, fifty per cent of the population, were very keen on the war. Before long they were wearing regimental badges, regimental buttons, little favours in their hats or coats, and they were offering to do the jobs men had done in civil life, so that men could be released. Some of them would stop us in the street and say, 'Well, why aren't you in khaki?' In other words the whole effect was cumulative, but we were not pressed, we made our own decisions.

Private F. B. Vaughan, Sheffield Pals

In August 1914, when the newsboys were running and shouting every day and all day, I was alone in the house, my family being at the seaside. I waited until they came back before I enlisted, in early September. Years later, I often asked myself why I had joined the Army. The usual explanations were no good. I was not hot with patriotic feeling; I did not believe that Britain was in any real danger. I was sorry for 'gallant little Belgium' but did not feel she was waiting for me to rescue her. The legend of Kitchener, who pointed at us from every hoarding, had never captured me. I was not under any pressure from public opinion, which had not got to work on young men as early as that; the white feathers came later. I was not carried to the recruiting office in a herd rush of chums, nobody thinking, everybody half-plastered; I went alone ... I was not simply swapping jobs; though the office bored me, life in the Army certainly did not attract me, and for some years I had regarded with contempt those lads who wanted to wear a uniform and be marched about. This was no escape to freedom and independence; I may not have known much about military life, but I was not so green. And I certainly did not see myself as a hero, whose true stature would be revealed by war; that had never been one of my illusions. What is left then to supply a motive? Nothing, I believe now, that was rational and conscious ... So early in September I joined, like a chump, the infantry – to be precise, the Duke of Wellington's West Riding Regiment, known in some circles as 'The Havercake Lads', in others as 'The Dirty Duke's'. I hurried along Market Street ... late again, for the last time. Instead of asking the boss if there was anything more, I shook his outstretched hand, then walked out of junior clerkdom forever. I reported at the regimental depot in Halifax, where a regular sergeant, noting sardonically the newish sports coat and flannel trousers that, like a fool, I was wearing, set me to work at once removing the congealed fat from immense cooking pots.

Private J. B. Priestley, 10th West Riding Regiment

I worked for the Sheffield Education Department. My friend Ned Muxlow who worked in the same office as me came in and said, 'Shall we go and enlist in the City Battalion?' I said 'Alright, we can go at dinner time' but he replied 'no, let's go now'. So I got my cap and went and signed on. Instead of getting the King's shilling we received 1s 6d. I don't know why and it's worried me ever since. I still spent it though!

Lance Corporal J. R. 'Reg' Glenn,
12th York and Lancaster (Sheffield City Battalion)

I saw this lot in the paper and it said it was all Leeds people, and I joined up, I didn't know what a soldier did … I didn't even know that the infantry walked to be quite truthful. I didn't know anything about soldiers … but it appealed to me and I went and I've never regretted a moment of it really, because I never met a finer lot of fellows in my life.

Private Arthur Dalby, Leeds Pals

For fourteen-year-old Frank Lindley, there was a more personal reason:

I lost my brother in one of the first ships to go down in the 'Big War'. Harry had come home from the Mediterranean Fleet exercises. He hadn't been home a few days when war broke out. They fetched him back, shoved him on a scratch cruiser HMS *Hawke* out in the North Sea and down they went, torpedoed. Me and my dad were getting ready to go to work one morning and a knock came at the door and there was a telegram, sudden, like that, October time. We read the bugger and we both collapsed. That finished my dad, he died in 1918 … I had itchy feet fired by Harry's travels. While he was on leave we used to talk because he used to sleep in the same bed. He said, 'Now Frank, I've got it all planned. We're refitting for the Far East and when I get to Australia I shall jump ship and go take a tract of land, then I'll send for you.'" That was the very last thing he said to me. We were pals me and him. We used to go all over. He even used to send money to clothe me. I had rather a posh job, a dental mechanic, and I used to have an appearance because I was dealing with titled people. That's what made me go to war, I wanted to avenge Harry's death.

Private Frank Lindley, Barnsley Pals

Caught up in the rush to volunteer in local units were other young men like Horace Iles of Leeds, also just fourteen when he managed to convince the Leeds Pals Raising Committee that he was old enough to enlist. Attestation papers, completed at enlistment, noted only a recruit's 'apparent age' and did not include a date of birth – largely because among the poorer classes from whom the army had traditionally taken its recruits papers like birth certificates were rarely kept. It was a criminal offence to knowingly make a false statement as to age but, as one manual explained,

OFFICER (to boy of thirteen who, in his effort to get taken on as a bugler, has given his age as sixteen): "Do you know where boys go who tell lies?"
APPLICANT: "To the Front, sir."

Attestation papers did not ask for a date of birth, only 'Apparent Age'. Many children were able to pass as older than they were.

It is recommended that as a rule a man should not be tried for making a false answer as to age, as it is considered that his age is not a fact within his own knowledge, and therefore it could not be proved that the answer was wilfully false. Lieutenant

Colonel S. T. Banning, *Military Law Made Easy.*

Boys like Iles were able to slip through the net because, in the rush to fill the ranks of the new battalions, shortcuts were taken in the process:

They were medically examined, I say it without fear of contradiction, in a most haphazard manner. Twenty to thirty per cent of the men were never medically examined at all … I knew of one doctor who medically examined 400 men a day for ten days and he didn't work twenty-four hours in a day.

Lt Col H. Clay, *Evidence to 1922 War Office Committee into Shell Shock*

Any medical man who could spare time to examine recruits was welcomed. These boys lined up naked against the walls of the Tram Offices. How I remember them! How anxious they were to join up! A whole bunch of them swerved over to the group of medical men because we were reacting few, and passing recruits in quickly. One drunken volunteer was turned out by an austere doctor who said the Army must not be degraded by 'drink'. However, the recruit came up again. I saw him enter the room, and in a few minutes he was in the Army. One old man who had been at Tel el Kebir came before me. When he was rejected as far too old he said, 'You'll want me before you've finished'. The examination was to me a strange one. Men who could jump and hop and shout, 'Who goes there ?' were thought by some examiners to be strong in wind and limb, strong enough to fight, while men with the classical faults of the recruiting tests, variocele flat foot, varicose veins, and the like, were rejected in large numbers. All these faults were subsequently ignored, and recruits who could shoot and march, whose internal organs were capable of bearing strain, were accepted. Undoubtedly in later days many men were admitted into the Army who were quite incapable of marching or fighting, who were indeed of no good to the Army, could not be of any good, and who were eventually rejected. In many cases they reached the Front only to be sent home. But in the early days, the men were on the whole the best men. If not always the best in physique, they were full of fine spirit.

The policeman Bretherick standing outside the street door of the Recruiting Office was a valuable recruiting agent. Bretherick was too old to enlist but he sent his son and son-in-law. He told the crowd of waiting lads this, and his eloquence was simple and direct. 'You've come here to enlist, and that's all you've come for, so march in!' And big lumps melted off the crowd and pushed through the door. Some were a little sheepish, some had flushed and some had pale faces; some were big, many were small. One thin lad was evidently suffering from phthisis – many were rejected on account of tuberculosis – 'I know I am,' he said to me, 'but I thought I should get in, I could do something.' As the months went by, it was evident that many unfit men had got in. I was able to compile a list of 167 who were known to the medical staff of the Tuberculosis Dispensary as tuberculous. Of these sixty to seventy were sent back during the first fifteen months, and fifty of them died. On the other hand, many sufferers from tuberculosis improved, even to the extent of apparent cure. In the Tuberculosis hospitals, the same furore to enlist was shown and many beds were emptied, the men slipping out and slipping in to the Army. Later, the nation and the Army came to regret this, but who could blame the fiery enthusiasts who took the patriotic course?

Dr H. de Carle Woodcock, Leeds

I was still an apprentice woolsorter so they sent me with some samples down to Bradford to different firms. As I'm coming back I call in at the recruiting

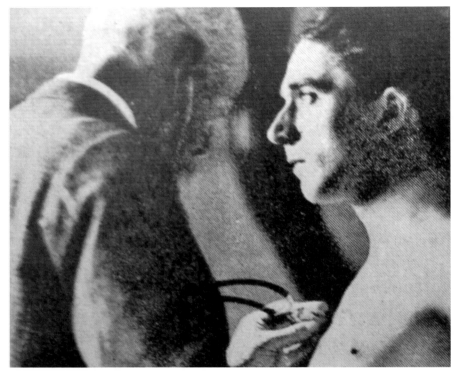

Army medical. Basic at the best of times, in 1914 it was often missed altogether.

office. I was only a lad, like. Anyway I go on the scale and I weigh 108lbs and the doctor says, Oh this fellow will swell out, so they passed me and I got a shilling. I went across to the Theatre De Luxe and had a right good time. I went back to work and told the boss, I'm in the Army, and he said 'Thank God we've got a Navy'.

Private Ernest Wilson, 18th West Yorkshires

Once passed by the medics, the next step was to swear the oath of allegiance:

The parson was there, he was called Huggard. He swore us in. We got six at a time holding the Bible and we had to hold it and repeat after him until we were sworn in. We got the King's shilling then we were dismissed for the day and told to report next morning. Naturally I went home. I'll always remember that night. They had all gone to bed except me and my dad. I was just going to bed and I just turned around and said, 'Goodnight Dad', and I can see him now. My mother had a sewing machine underneath the window sill and he was standing there with his hand on the sewing machine. He said 'Goodnight lad but just think on, after tonight you're not always forced to have a bed to go to'. I remembered those words many a time in the next three of four years.

Private Tommy Oughton, Barnsley Pals

With little else to do, the newly enlisted Pals went home to await further instruction. In August alone, 298,923 men enlisted. In September, the creation of the Pals battalions and news of the retreat from Mons brought another 462,901 recruits but recruiting rapidly tailed off. After weeks without any sign of the threatened German invasion, the initial rush had subsided and new methods of drumming up recruits were tried:

The illuminated tram car was out and about blazing its electrical devices in deadly earnest during the dark evenings of November, for it had become apparent that the credit of the city was at stake; the Leeds roll of recruits

Swearing the oath of allegiance.

The Leeds recruiting tram.

at this stage still fell short of the numbers recorded at one or two other populous centres.

William Herbert Scott

At the bottom of the park, just there it came, and I was only a schoolgirl, and we went down to see this lovely tram. There was a big military man, he stood upstairs like on the top deck, that was open, and he was going with his arms, pleading with them, 'We need you, we need you!' All the crowds were watching and when he'd finished all the young men that were watching got on that tram, went inside and enlisted, and I often wondered whether any of them got killed…

Marjorie Took, Leeds

Meanwhile, the Territorials who had marched away to camp to prepare for active service soon found full time soldiering was very different to the experience of summer camps:

It was frightful at Strensall. The tents were overcrowded and we were starved of all kinds of essential supplies, never mind kit and uniforms. I had to wear fatigue dress until I got my khaki. There were no tables to sit at at meal times, there was no cutlery and we got all our meal together in one go in one billy-can – stew, a hunk of bread, a lump of cheese, a dollop of jam, all mixed up together. I could not stomach it at all. It was a terrible shock to someone like me who had had such a refined upbringing with nice meals and a servant to put them in front of me.

Private Brian Armitage, Leeds Rifles

A prevalent complaint was homesickness. Short leave to visit Bradford was given freely, and the mistaken kindness of relatives and friends made the crime of overstaying leave a popular one. I well remember one lad who was brought up in the Orderly Room for absence without leave and whose excuse was that he had gone to the station to see one of his friends off, and the sight of a train marked 'Bradford' had been too much for his budding sense of military discipline.

Colonel H. O. Wade, 6th West Yorkshires

Beginning to find Strensall rather a dead hole. No amusements except those made by ourselves. It is quite a common sight to see grown men playing marbles with the zest of schoolboys. There is a picture house of sorts which is worth a visit to see and hear the antics and jokes of the audience.

Sergeant W. B. Burrell, Leeds Rifles

There were, however, the occasional breaks to the routine:

What excitement! Order received at 10 a.m.: 'Be prepared to move at short notice'. We heard unofficially that the German Fleet was off Lowestoft and that we were off to repel a landing. Everything was quickly packed and we awaited the 'Move' order. At 6.30 p.m . an order was received cancelling the move. Oh, the gnashing of teeth! We unpacked. Brought out of bed at 10.30 p.m. to repack – the move was on again! Stood by all night – only to have the move again cancelled. Too tired to swear.

Sergeant W. B. Burrell, Leeds Rifles, 'Diary Entry', 3 November 1914

Unbeknown to the bored men at Strensall Camp, the German Navy had been seeking opportunities to draw out small sections of the British fleet which it could then trap and destroy in the North Sea. A German submarine, the U-17, had been sent to investigate the defences along the coast between Scarborough and Hartlepool – both listed as

B Company of the Leeds Pals at the start of their training at Colsterdale.

Lack of uniforms meant that early training was completed in the suits the men had enlisted in.

'defended towns' in maritime guides of the time – and reported back that there were no minefields within 12 miles of the shore but there was a steady stream of shipping. A fleet was assembled and sailed to a position just off Dogger Bank, ready to engage British ships as they responded to the planned raid.

On the morning of 16 December, the German battle cruisers *Seydlitz*, *Blücher* and *Moltke* headed toward Hartlepool, while the *Derfflinger*, *Von der Tann* and *Kolberg* approached Scarborough. At 0815, *Kolberg* started laying mines off Flamborough Head while the *Derfflinger* and *Von der Tann* began shelling the town in a ninety minute bombardment before moving off to Whitby.

'The Germans are landing! The Germans are landing!' I did not feel apprehensive or excited. I just felt that the time I'd trained for had come and I was quite calm and quite prepared for anything that might have been going to happen.

Private Thomas Darbyshire, 8th West Yorkshires,
Hospital patient in Scarborough when the attack began

The bombardment morning was December 16; I was seven years and five days old. It was a misty morning. We were up early before school. And my mother was in the act of putting the porridge out for us onto the plates when the first shell cracked. My mother said, 'Oh, what's that noise?' My father said 'It's gunfire, it'll be alright it'll be some of our ships practising.' Never dreamt it would be Germans. As soon as it was over I went out and went round the corner to see if school was still there – unfortunately it was!

Sydney Smith

Suddenly at 9.10 a.m. we heard what the children thought was blasting, only very near, the windows rattled and the house shook again and again. I said 'I am sure it's firing off the coast'... I can tell you the sound was pretty terrifying but it only lasted ten minutes, the car was ordered and away we flew to Whitby. We were there about three-quarters of an hour after the two German cruisers had gone but the houses they had wrecked were awful. When we got near Whitby we saw streams of people with panic stricken faces trying to get away. I never want to see such a thing again ... Telegraph wires hanging like threads all snapped, huge gaping holes in the side of houses, roofs off, glass smashed everywhere and old women shaking with fright and sobbing. We picked up lots of bits of shell. I have one in my pocket as I write. The two German cruisers fired at the coastguard station, shot that to bits and killed one coastguard; we saw the stretcher being carried. Some of the coastguards said the cruisers came in so close they could see the men

Scarborough under fire.

working on their decks. We hear that these cruisers have visited Scarborough and other places and damaged them, but as all wires are out of order it is difficult to get news. In one street the venetian blinds had been blown right across the street, lamp post upturned and I saw a pool of blood in front of a house so went in to see if anyone was hurt. We found that an old woman had been hit by a shell and was bleeding badly and was removed to the hospital. The extraordinary thing was so few were killed or even badly hurt. Portions of furniture, doors and windows were lying about the streets, and in the fields just outside the town are large holes about five or six feet square. If the shells had been fired earlier when people were in bed I should think hundreds would have been killed as so many of the bedrooms were struck.

Colina Campbell, twenty-three-year-old Voluntary Aid
Detachment nurse, December 1914

A news blackout was imposed as terrified refugees took the first available trains out of town. As the nearest force, the Leeds Rifles were called forward to meet the attack:

What a sensation this caused. The battalion nearly went mad with delight at the prospect of a scrap … the men were in the highest spirits as we marched to the railway station, and the crowds who lined the streets to see us off nearly went mad with excitement.

Bandsman John Sanderson, Leeds Rifles

By the time they arrived in the town, the raid was over and their job became one of restoring order and confidence in the frightened townsfolk. For one family, though, the morning was memorable for a different reason:

THE SHRAPNEL BABY. WHITBY CHILD BORN UNDER SHELL FIRE.

Just as the German cruisers opened fire on Whitby on the morning of Wednesday December 16, Mrs. Edward Griffin, wife of a local ship-yard worker, gave birth to her seventh child, a son.

She was at her home in The Crag, a row of small tenements on the west bank of the Esk, directly in the line of fire. The mother well understood the meaning of the crash of the guns and shrapnel, and feared that any moment a shell might wreck the house, but, fortunately, The Crag escaped.

The boy has now been christened George after the King, and Shrapnel in memory of the bombardment. His father is notable locally, having saved thirty-six people from drowning, and holding the Royal Humane Society's bronze medal and certificate. The facts attending the birth were brought to the notice of the King, who has written expressing his pleasure that the mother and child escaped injury, and congratulating the father upon his magnificent life-saving record.

Daily Graphic, December 1915

The attack had killed 137 people and wounded another 592. Although Hartlepool had been hit most heavily, it was the attack on the resort town of Scarborough that most shocked the nation. 'Remember Scarborough' became a rallying call for recruiters. British homes had come under enemy fire for the first time in centuries. It was now very clear this would be a war unlike any other.

3

1915:
'NO MORE WONDERFUL AND EVENTFUL YEAR'

The declaration of war with the best customer of the wool and textile trades of this country was a blow which staggered every section of the industry, and for the time being no-one knew what to do.

Bradford Weekly Telegraph, 1 January 1915

There were fears that the industry – of such vital importance to Leeds – might not recover from the emphatic check of war. It's 'good time', however, was not long in coming. Army orders soon gave ample employment. Contracts for boots, and for khaki cloth, too, rolled in. The early queues of workless grew smaller and smaller. Trade prospects all round brightened, though it meant a diversion of ways and means and some considerable adaptation to the novelty of the industrial situation.

William Herbert Scott, 1922

On the declaration of war ... The future of the cotton trade aroused considerable anxiety for a time, and it was curious how far out in their reckoning most of the prophets were in this respect. The general opinion was that trade would be paralysed, leading to a period of great privation; but these fears were soon found to be without foundation. Work was more abundant, and wages higher, in most trades, than ever before, due partly to the scarcity of labour, but more particularly to the grant of increased wages to meet the higher cost of living. In anticipation of the expected hard times, Relief Committees were appointed and Relief Funds opened, and a movement was organised for the feeding of necessitous School children.

This latter movement grew to such dimensions that for the week ending 25 September the number of children being supplied with free meals was 560; but by the following January conditions had so far altered that the number of so-called necessitous children on the books had fallen to eleven.

John A. Lee, Todmorden

At the start of 1915, businesses in the West Riding began to take stock of recent events. Fears of a catastrophic economic collapse had quickly been replaced by a recognition that the rapidly expanding Army offered more than enough work to go around since every soldier would need a uniform and weapons to fight with. A shortage of khaki cloth meant that initially, stocks of blue serge would be used:

Local industry has received further big support by an enquiry from the War Office authorities for 15,000 pieces of blue serge cloth, to be delivered at the rate of 500 pieces a day. The Lord Mayor, Alderman John Arnold, was asked to place the orders and he immediately had enquiries made of merchants and manufacturers as to what quantity of suitable material they had ... The Chamber of Commerce was also acquainted by the Lord Mayor of the order and the members communicated with, indicating that the government were prepared to buy, through the Lord Mayor, a large quantity of serges.

Clayton Times and Express, 11 September 1914.

In Bradford, the formation of what would become three battalions of Bradford Pals meant order books quickly filled:

The serious work of arranging contracts for the clothing of the Bradford Service Battalion ... has now been completed, and stipulations have been made for quick delivery. Tenders have been accepted as follows: Greatcoats, Messrs Wright Burrows, Burrows & Co., Huddersfield; jackets and trousers, divided between Mr David Murie (Bradford), Mr R. Mettrick (Guisley), Miller, Rayner & Haysom Limited (London) and Messrs George Brown & Son (Bradford); puttees, Messrs Fox & Todd (Bradford); regulation Army caps, Brown, Muff & Co. Limited (Bradford). The whole of the serge for the jackets and trousers is Bradford made and the lustre lining and other linings are from Bradford houses. The puttees are made in Bradford. The buttons – a great source of difficulty – have been specially made to Government pattern by a Bradford firm.

Yorkshire Observer, 23 October 1914

Soldiers also needed to eat and, just as important, something to eat with. Sheffield cutlers rushed to meet the demand:

The firms who are not participating in the boom are exceptional, as anyone can dispose of the whole of their stocks of a suitable pattern.

Sheffield Telegraph, 4 September 1914

Stocks of khaki dye ran low since before the war they had been imported from Germany but alternatives were found. Picric acid, a yellow dye, could be combined with others to produce an acceptable khaki but more importantly, it could also be used in the manufacture of Lyddite, an explosive widely used in munitions. Skilled dye-workers, used to handling the volatile substance, found themselves in demand in the munitions factories opening across the county. Business in the West Riding was, quite literally, booming – although not always for the best:

At about 2 p.m. on 2 December 1914, an explosion ripped through the acid works of Henry Ellison Limited on Hollinbank Lane, Heckmondwike where fifteen men were working. Frederick Wright, a chemist from Cleckheaton, James Nicholas, a foreman from White Lee, brothers Albert and Nimrod Firth, Percy Ashton, Clifford Thornton of Heckmondwike, John Edward Morton, a labourer from Staincliffe, George Terry, a labourer from White Lee, J. Arthur Cooper, a mason's labourer from Heckmondwike and William Berry, of Low Moor were all killed as the blast sent a huge yellow cloud high over the scene. The task of identifying the victims was carried out by the police and workmen and was a very distressing proceeding. A large number of people at first surged round the bodies, for what reason it seemed difficult to conjecture, for the spectacle presented was, to say the least, horrible, and naturally the task was somewhat distasteful to those compelled to undertake it.

Spenborough Guardian, December 1914

The bodies recovered were described as mutilated beyond recognition, and some had to be identified by the contents of their pockets. The factory itself was reduced to rubble and pieces of machinery were scattered in surrounding fields, nearby houses destroyed and local residents injured, leaving the area 'looking as if it had been visited by the German Army'. Hundreds of windows were broken and many homes left uninhabitable. The cause of the blast was never confirmed but at the inquest into the deaths, the coroner blamed a spark from a grinding machine and cast doubts on the safety standards at the factory, which had only been back in operation for six weeks before the disaster. Despite such setbacks, though, it was widely seen as a good time for local business:

There has been no more wonderful and eventful year than that which is just drawing to a close in the whole history of the woollen industry.

Yorkshire Observer, 31 December 1914

Success was a double-edged sword. Britain needed a large Army but it also needed workers to supply it. In the patriotic fervour that had gripped the nation, every man of military age was coming under pressure to enlist every time he ventured into the street and many men whose skills meant they were of more use at home had already left work to join up. In some areas young women had taken to handing out white feathers as symbols of cowardice to men in the street – rarely if ever considering there might be a reason they were not in uniform. Highly skilled technicians essential to the supply of weapons and ammunition were humiliated by being told they should do their bit for the war effort. Men who had tried to enlist but had been rejected and even discharged soldiers, physically unfit due to their wounds, were sometimes targeted. In response, the government began to issue armbands and badges to workers it considered vital. In some cases, soldiers were either discharged or posted back to their old jobs but now working in uniform. In Liverpool, an entire battalion of the Liverpool Regiment was formed in order to keep dockers at home. Men signing up for it received special terms:

He will engage to serve His Majesty as a soldier in a Dock Battalion of the Liverpool Regiment in the United Kingdom for the duration of the war, at the end of which he will be discharged with all convenient speed … [he] will be paid the Infantry pay of [his] rank, and in addition will receive transport pay at the rates recognised by the Joint Labour Committee of the Port of Liverpool, such transport pay to be in no case less than 35s a week, unless on any day they have failed to parade in accordance with Regimental Orders.

'Terms of Enlistment' from the service record of
2242 Frederick John Adams, of Docks Battalion, Liverpool Regiment

As more and more men left for the forces, positions opened up for women to start to enter the workplace in large numbers. Arguments from trade unions and others about the ability of women to cope with industrial work ignored the fact that only seventy years earlier, the Mines and Collieries Act of 1842 had only banned women from working underground in the pits and many women and girls in the coalfield areas still worked long, hard hours in surface jobs. Munitions work offered good rates of pay and larger factories even offered hostels and pre-fabricated homes for families, attracting women from across the region.

Industry was affected as men rushed to the colours and so some were released by the army or posted back as soldiers to their old job.

Oh they all came in, the women, then. Well, they worked the lathes, the machines. They did quite a few jobs, the womenfolk that came in. Well they weren't as skilled as the men that'd been brought up with the job, but they did just the job that they were told to do. And there were more repetition work then than previously in the years before the war. Well, some didn't – the older men didn't like it, but some enjoyed it because they, some went to have a drink at night with them, but not me.

Harry Smith

It wasn't what you'd call a healthy job. Because, well, at that time my hair was jet black and I used to have to bend over the boshes with the acid. You've seen the style today where people have their hair bleached at the front well my hair went like that, just at the front with bending over the boshes where the acid was, because we used to have to put the tubes in this hot acid. Well the hot tubes used to make the acid hot and then the fumes used to come up. It was a very unhealthy job but nevertheless I was very happy there.

Beatrice Lee, Yorkshire Copper Works

Suffragists saw the war as an opportunity to demonstrate that they, too, could help the war effort.

Munitions workers.

We had to stem … the powder into shells with broom handles and mallets. You see, you'd have your shell and the broom handle, your tin of powder. And you'd put a bit in, stem it down, put a bit more in, stem it down. It took you all your time to get it all in. It was very hard work.

Elsie McIntyre, Barnbow Munitions Factory in Leeds

We found work then at the [factory]. And it turned out to be a TNT factory – TNT. And you all had to change when you went in. You had to strip and change into other clothes because you weren't allowed a little tiny bit of metal on you at all, not one hook or eye or anything. And of course they had corsets in those days with wires in them, you see. And you had to finish up with an overall and put your head covering on. And they used to give us domes of glass on the table with holes for your hands to go through, and you filled up the gains. Gains were something like cartridges but bigger. You filled them up with this black rock stuff. And everyone turned yellow there. And you washed so that the yellow came off, but it was always in your system.

Kathleen Gilbert

Soon, the ever-present yellow dye seeped into their clothes, skin and eyes so that munitions workers could easily be distinguished in any crowd and earned the nickname 'Canaries'. Although wages for canaries were high, it reflected the demands put on girls as young as fifteen:

[Can I ask] the Secretary of State for the Home Department whether his attention has been drawn to the legal prosecution of a firm of engineers engaged at cartridge-making in Armley, Leeds, in which it was shown that a girl under eighteen years of age worked from 6 a.m. on Friday till 7 a.m. on Saturday, when she met with an accident, while an older woman worked from 6 a.m. on Friday till 11 a.m. on Saturday; whether he is aware that the Stipendiary Magistrate declined to convict on the ground that he might be limiting the output of ammunition; whether his attention has also been drawn to the death from exhaustion of an artificer at the Small Arms Factory, Enfield, who was stated to have worked eighty and a-half hours a week since August, thirty-two hours a week above normal; and whether he can take steps in co-operation with the military and naval authorities to encourage only such industrial conditions as will not destroy physical health and in the end retard output?

William Anderson, MP for Sheffield,
House of Commons, 28 April 1915

By January 1915, 1.2 million men had enlisted into an army geared towards accepting just 30,000 recruits a year. The regimental depots were swamped and for a time, no-one seemed quite sure what to do with the eager volunteers:

You were more or less at liberty at first, as long as you were there for parade next morning. We used to come home three or four nights a week, as long as we caught the first train back in the morning. There was a train at half past seven from Wombwell.

Private Harry Hall, 13th York and Lancaster Regiment

At first, the Barnsley Pals slept in a hall in the town centre:

I had to stop any suspicious characters from entering the hall, but most of the suspicious ones were already inside. There was a big rubber mat that covered the whole entrance and I fell asleep on it. The next thing I knew there was somebody kicking me - it was a policeman and he wanted to know what I was doing there. I told him that I was supposed to be guarding the Public Hall.

Private Harry Hall, 13th York and Lancaster Regiment

With no uniforms, equipment or even trained instructors, the Pals battalions were forced to improvise. Training grounds were found for them wherever land could be made available. The Barnsley Pals had to build their own camp from scratch and facilities were basic to begin with. The beds, in particular, left something to be desired:

We had three flat boards on trestles and mattresses full of straw. As a rule two of you used to get down together to make a double. You each had two blankets, so when you got together you'd put one on the bottom and three on top. Me and Tom Bradbury kipped like that. We had a proper hut for meals and a cookhouse. Of course when we first got there the Barnsley British Co-Operative Society was still feeding us. I expect that it all came out of the government later on, but they catered for us. You could see the big vans coming out of Barnsley every day. I heard many men say, men older than me who were married, that they were better fed than in civilian life.

Private Tommy Oughton, 13th York and Lancaster Regiment

Lacking basic amenities, the camps also lacked any sort of organisation:

We went there [to Colsterdale in North Yorkshire] we had no NCOs, no lance corporals and corporals. They'd sergeants, Reserve men forty or fifty years of age you see, but they knew the job. So we'd to find some NCOs. Mind you, it didn't just happen to the Leeds Pals, it happened all over because they'd a million men in no time, you know, and it takes some working.

Private Clifford Hollingworth, Leeds Pals

Men who had any experience of drill and discipline in Boys Brigade, Boy Scouts etc were asked to step forward and see what sort of army NCOs they might make.

Private Arthur Pearson, Leeds Pals

To begin with, men paraded in their own civilian suits:

One quaint, but useless sergeant was very perturbed at having no uniform. He was only a sergeant because at some time or another, probably in a previous existence, he had been in the Army, and consequently knew the words of command. His dress consisted of a bowler hat (which was not in the heyday of youth), a starched collar (the only one he had, and after three weeks it was looking a trifle tired), a dickey, but no tie, a black waistcoat and a black tailcoat, a pair of nondescript trousers and an ancient pair of brown boots … It was no wonder that (as he complained to me) the men did not realise his position.

Unofficial war record of the 9th KOYLI

Training for Kitchener's army.

Heads up and shoulders back, cold water washes, cold water shaves and plenty of good food, we were soon fit as fiddles. The natty gent's suiting in which we lived and moved and had our being soon began to show that they had not been made to stand the rough wear that they were getting. We looked more like tramps every day as we bust our jackets and tore our trousers. Scarves began to take the place of collars and ties, even though some of these collars were made of celluloid which would wash with a lick.

Private Arthur Pearson, Leeds Rifles

Hopping around a field, first on one leg and then on another, may seem almost a ridiculous procedure and one very far remote from the supreme object of killing Germans, but it has a very real place in the long preparations of the true soldier and the Leeds men are taking it up with enthusiasm, as a course of training which they recognise is good for them.

Yorkshire Post, 28 September 1914

Another form of training that would stand them in good stead in the years to come was the art of route marching:

Route marching was the big thing and I was taking size ten boots when I joined up. I can remember going home once with bad feet, they were giving me some stick. My dad asked what the matter was and when I told him that the boots were killing me, he said, 'I'll get thee a pair of boots'. Off he went and got me a pair with soft tops. He took mine to use at the pit. We used to march out as far as Kexborough and on the way back along Wakefield Road we'd have a stop at 'The Sportsman' Smithies. Tommy Guest used to have a barrel laid on outside. There'd be a pint for all of us – he was a good old stick!

Private Harry Hall, 13th York and Lancaster Regiment

On one march we were passing a road sweeper, who must have been an old soldier. He looked up and did a marvellous present arms with his broom, and our officer returned the salute.

Lance Corporal J. R. Glenn, Sheffield Pals

With khaki cloth in short supply, surplus post office blue material was made available. The issue of a uniform of sorts helped the recruits to feel a little more military but unfortunately, not everyone recognised it for what it was:

The battalion was on a route march one day and was passing through the village of Bamford in Derbyshire. Two old ladies were standing at the side of the road watching us go by. One was overheard to say to the other, 'Ee it must be a terrible war if they have to turn out convicts to fight in it!'

Private Herbert Hall, Sheffield Pals

I remember once marching through Stairfoot, we were in our blues at the time. There were some youngsters coming running to see us and I heard one voice shout 'Oi! Come on there's some soldiers here'. And then another voice called out 'Oh, it's only t'Barnsley Battalion'.

Private Tommy Oughton, 13th York and Lancaster Regiment

If conditions for the Pals seemed grim, some of the Territorial Force felt even more hard done by. The Territorials had been ordered to 'recruit to wartime strength, then double'. The plan was that each battalion would recruit the 1,000 men needed to bring it up to strength and then to continue until it had 2,000. Then each battalion would split, creating, for example, the 1/5th and the 2/5th Battalions. The 'first line' 1/5th would then take the experienced men into action, leaving the 'second line' 2/5th to train and prepare to follow on. Life in a second line Territorial unit seemed bleak:

Unlike units of the New Army, the second line Territorials had to fend for themselves. They received no specially skilled instructors to help with training, they were practically without uniforms and equipment, they had no such luxuries as field kitchen, bands, blue uniforms presented to them by grateful cities; on the contrary everything was made as difficult as possible for them. Their best men were sent to the first line in return for 'unfits'; they were not allowed to recruit until Kitchener's army had obtained the best men; they had to take on training grounds that were not required by other units ... The general impression was one of neglect, they seemed nobody's darlings.

Captain E. C. Gregory, 2/5th West Yorkshires

Training for Kitchener's army.

Leaving the second line units and the Pals battalions to continue training, the first line Territorials had been training hard and by April 1915, they were ready to be sent overseas. The terms of their enlistment meant that they could not be ordered to go – every man was a volunteer who had signed the Imperial Service Obligation to agree to be posted abroad. Most assumed they would be sent to garrison duties in far-flung corners of empire to free up regular battalions and so had accepted the invitation to sign. Not all did. Arthur Green wrote to his father to ask permission:

During the day everyone has been signing up their papers for Foreign Service. The bulk of the men are keen and as far as I can see I appear to be the only officer not to have signed … I should love to have a trip abroad with these chaps; we could not be ready for service in under three or four months, the only chance we have is to be sent to relieve some garrison at Gibraltar or Malta or some such place and there is no distinction between Colonial and Foreign service. If you don't want me to go out then I've nothing more to say.

Second Lieutenant Arthur Green,
5th West Yorkshires, September 1914

Clearly, Lieutenant Green's father did not agree, leading to a second letter:

[I wanted] to ask if you were willing for me to sign the Imperial Service Form which will render me liable for service anywhere. I can't see any possibility of being sent out to France, with things as black as they are now, a Zeppelin invasion at any time or an army invasion will require the Territorials to stay at home. Then, owing to not having volunteered I have been sent to the reserve battalion where we are drilling the rawest recruits and we have not even touched a rifle yet and who cannot possibly be ready for use before February or March so I can't see any possibility of going abroad, either to the colonies or to France. But still, at the same time, I feel that if the call did come later on in the war – I should not quite be playing the game if I smugly hid behind the excuse of 'home service' and refuse to go away with the officers I have grown up with, and with the men whom I am doing my best to prepare for the worst.

Second Lieutenant Arthur Green,
2/5th West Yorkshires, September 1914

By then a frustrated Captain, Arthur Green, would finally reach France with the battalion in 1917. Meanwhile, the first line Territorials had spent the past months in intensive training around Doncaster:

Ranges at Cantley and Scunthorpe were used. A little trench digging was done near Armthorpe but, as it was still hoped that the war would soon become one of movement again, this form of training was not taken very seriously.

Captain P. G. Bales, 1/4th Duke of Wellington's Regiment

At half-past five in the afternoon on Monday April 12th, 1915, the first detachment of troops in the West Riding (1st Line) Territorial Division left England for France. Their going, like all English goings and most English home-comings, was quiet and unobserved: the War Diary of the Division merely states that 'thus the move to France commenced'; further, that Divisional Headquarters left Doncaster the next day, embarked at Folkestone on the Invicta, and reached Boulogne 9.50 p.m. that the General Officer Commanding the Division, accompanied by five Staff Officers, travelled by motor-car on April 14 through St. Orner and Hazebroucke to Merville where Divisional Headquarters were established in the Mayor's house, 40 rue des Capucines; and that a telegram was received by the General from H. R. the King and a loyal reply was despatched. So, the time of preparation was over. The time of action had begun.

L. Magnus, *West Riding Territorials in the Great War*

For the majority of men this was the furthest they had ever travelled, although arrival in France was sometimes a disappointment since French docks looked almost identical to the ones they had just left, and only careful searching revealed the signs and notices that proved this was a foreign country.

I was in France, grass grew in France, just like it did in England – it was the same colour. I looked down on Boulogne. It was a lovely morning but mist covered most of the town, with church spires and towers sticking through it. As the mist cleared Boulogne revealed itself. Across the town we could see the English Channel and across that – but not to be seen – was HOME. I had become a member of the British Expeditionary Force.

Private Phil Brockleby, 9th York & Lancaster, 27 August 1915

Thoughts turned to what lay ahead:

The thought of getting killed or wounded never once occurred to me, but I felt greatly worried as to how I should behave under fire and I don't mind confessing here that I was very much afraid I might do something to disgrace myself. In other words, now that I was getting near to the real thing I didn't feel quite sure of myself, though previously I had been one of the most eager.

Bandsman John Sanderson, Leeds Rifles

Soon, letters arrived home describing their first experiences:

We went into the trenches for the first time on Monday. The worst part about it is getting in and out under fire more or less for about 600 yards. Once you get in it is safe as houses … I wish we had been staying a week or two – it's a birthday! So long as you keep careful there is no danger at all except from a stray shot or so. Don't know when we are going in again but I hope it won't be long … I can tell you I enjoyed it.

Private Fred Wigglesworth, 1/7th West Yorkshire Regiment

Once there you are comparatively safe. It is the going in and out that is the sport. My feelings in the trenches were not at all as I expected. I really enjoyed it … It was all very fascinating, and after the first hour you did not feel that there was any danger at all.

Captain Douglas B. Winter, 1/4th Duke of Wellington's Regiment

We went into the trenches last Sunday evening until Wednesday evening. The Germans were about 250 yards from us. Never saw one of them but sent plenty of bullets over. About 200 yards at the back of us were some fruit trees in full bloom. A thrush sings there every day. Sparrows hop about near us for food. Larks and swallows are very numerous. I thought the gun and rifle fire would have scared them away. The other day I saw a big cat strolling down the road toward the firing line…

Private Alfred Sharman, 1/4th West Riding Regiment, Halifax

At last I have been under fire. We went into the trenches on Sunday night for twenty-four hours, and I would not have minded if it had been for twenty-four days. It was quite exciting – my first time under fire, you know … I only wish that we were going in tonight again.

Private Harry Pemberton, Leeds Rifles

I have never regretted the step I took when I first joined the Army and am glad that I have had the chance given to me to do my little bit for my country. I am thoroughly enjoying myself here and the thought that we are fighting for a cause that is right is a grand feeling … The last time we were in the trenches we gave the Germans a concert every day just to let them know the lads from Halifax can sing (or at least make a noise) as well as shoot.

Private Allan Millner, 1/4th West Riding Regiment,
'Letter to his Employer'

A British unit prepares to move into the trenches, 1915.

We were all of us surprised to find trench warfare and trench life so different from what we had expected. We had none of us imagined that the trenches could be so comfortable or so entirely safe as we found them … We found out afterwards that the first impressions were a little too favourable as the trenches into which we first went were by no means representative, but considerably safer, more comfortable and cleaner than the ordinary.

Lieutenant A. G. Rigby, 1/8th West Yorkshires

Lieutenant Rigby and the rest of the Leeds Rifles were given a gradual introduction to trench warfare by working alongside a regular battalion of the Scots Guards who had been in France for some time. It included such mundane tasks as how to maintain the trench by carrying out repairs:

This is one of those little jobs that do not shine in the reports, but it involves the maximum amount of risk with the minimum amount of honour.

Sergeant Angus MacFarlane, 1/8th West Yorkshires

The Scots Guards sergeant told me to look over the parapet. I was a bit leery about this, but he told me to go on and do it. I expected hundreds of bullets to come whizzing straight at me, but not even one did, and I couldn't see a single German. It was very disappointing.

Private Jack Barker, 1/7th West Yorkshires

After stand-to and breakfast I was able to get a better idea of the surroundings. I was enjoying myself immensely. I had a feeling of elation at the thought that I was here, only 200 yards or so from the German troops, and no-one between us … We were relieved that night and marched back to our billets at La Gorgue in higher spirits than ever. We sang every song we could think of at the tops of our voices. Were we not now real warriors, fighting soldiers proved and tried? In our ignorance we thought we knew all about warfare now.

Bandsman John Sanderson, Leeds Rifles

Writing home in July, one man described the events of his day:

ONE DAY'S LIFE IN THE TRENCHES

It was one of those sharpe [sic] crisp morning's in July, when the birds were singing their best. This morning however turned out to be a very Hot day still the birds would fly around as much as to say never mind boy's we will be happy, and still there were guns Howling as the shells they came over whistling that awful tune distruction. This was the day that our loyal comrades on our left known as the 5th York and Lancs (5th Y&L) belonging to 49th West Riding Division, it was here alas when their looses were great the German artillery distroyed life as easily as you would throw a burnt match to the ground, to the dismay of all, was [there], the Germans have taken the Y&L Trenches but not for long, reserves who were in the reserve Billets came along, through the reserve trenches across the pontoon Bridges & on to the Yser canal banks the reserves consisted of the 4th KOYLI and the 4th York and Lancs ready to do or die all fear had by now left the boys, one disire now was to retake at all cost. This did not last long the Trenches and dugouts were destroyed, our only gain was our firm position of the line we nearly lost, all arround was the dead, dying & wounded, some beyond Recognition. The Germans were buried as kindly as our own were laid to rest, It so Happened that this day of hell played with human life as if it were a piece of coal burning on your fires at home, this day was my last on the Yser cannal it was here I received my wound in the leg, it was just like a pin prick, caused by a piece of shrapnel as big as your hand, which dug into the ground, to my amazement my Captain who was by my side being Captain J. Walker. He spoke to me saying whats wrong Nobby. I said I Have been Hit sir, He said where but it wanted no looking for, where the shrapnel Hit me it had ripped my trouser's open the Captain took me into his dugout, and put his great coat under my leg so as to ease the blood from flowing so freely from the wound when some one shouted *** [indecipherable] killed. He went to Him saying as he went I will get you some bandage and see to it your knee when I come back, while He was away, Leut Acthinson came into the Captains dugout, smilled and said what have you been doing I only smilled at him, because he said to me earlier in the day I should get hit before the day is out a few minutes passed on when I remarked sir, I should be better in my own dug out He replied all right if you think you can manage, I got up dazed never the less I got to my own little [place].

Harold W. Clark, 1/5th KOYLI, July 1915

As the Territorials settled in to their new home in France, life for some of their former neighbours back home became even harder.

On 1 May 1915, the Cunard liner *RMS Lusitania* set sail from New York bound for Liverpool with almost 2,000 passengers and crew aboard. The German Embassy had published warnings in the New York papers for American citizens not to sail with her as she was now designated an 'auxiliary cruiser' by the German navy, who claimed she was carrying war supplies in contravention of the so-called 'Cruiser Rules' and therefore a legitimate target for their submarine patrols. At about 2.10 p.m. on 7 May, 11 miles off the coast of Ireland, the *Lusitania* sailed into the path of

An attack on German owned property during the *Lusitania* riots.

U-20, a U-Boat under the command of Kapitänleutnant Walther Schweiger, who launched a single torpedo which struck the ship on the starboard side. Moments later, a second explosion inside the ship blasted out her hull. Eighteen minutes later, the *Lusitania's* bow hit the seabed while her stern was still above water. Of the 1,959 passengers and crew, 1,195 died.

News of the sinking provoked outrage. In Liverpool, rioting broke out as German-owned businesses came under attack. In the coming days, violence spread to other towns and cities around the country. As in Keighley the previous year, the trouble began with an attack on German butchers by drunken locals. In Mexborough, a shop belonging to George Schonhut was attacked while in Goldthorpe, brothers George and Robert Milner decided to avenge the *Lusitania* by attacking the shop of his cousin Frederick Schohnhut – a local councillor born in Goole, claiming that 'in addition to rejoicing over the disaster to the *Lusitania*, F. Schonhut had also been ill-using his wife and sending bundles of hams away with messages inside'. In the aftermath, twenty-three rioters appeared at Leeds Assizes and the story of the riot reached the papers. During the attack on Schonhut's home and shop, a group had also attacked the London Tea and Drapery Stores owned by John Bakewell, a man described in court as having 'not a drop of German blood in his veins'. Bakewell himself was hit on the head by a brick and £3,000 worth of damage was done to his property. Worse, during the attack a shot was fired at the mob, and twenty-seven-year-old Jack Fades was killed.

On Friday 14 May, 1915, rioters attacked the premises of various pork butchers in Attercliffe, Sheffield, including those of George Hannemann. The following night police were stoned and a pitched battle broke out in Rotherham near the Red Lion Inn, owned by Tennant Brothers of Sheffield, but kept shortly before by one of the Schonhut family. On 18 May, it was the turn of George Limbach to have his premises destroyed by rioters.

A few months later, George Schonhut, whose shop at Mexborough had been destroyed on 10 May, was summoned at Doncaster for failing to register as an enemy alien, despite having served in the 1890s in the Queen's Own Yorkshire Dragoons, reaching the rank of sergeant and being chosen to represent the regiment at Queen Victoria's Diamond Jubilee. Back in 1891, he had been told by a solicitor that 'having taken the oath of allegiance [on joining the forces] it was not necessary to go through the form of naturalisation'. The advice was wrong. He was fined £5, and lost his seat on the Mexborough Urban Council. Meanwhile, Wilhelm Schonhut, a student born in Parkgate, Rotherham and another member of the same family, had been interned in Germany where he was regarded as being British. In October 1916, George Schonhut's twenty-six-year old son was conscripted into the British army.

In Hull, the Hohenrein family became the target for the mob:

Dear Sir, I belong to a secret gang but want to be your friend. I wish to warn you that your shop's in danger and perhaps life for God's sake take this as a warning from one who wishes you no harm (Don't treat this as an idel [sic] joke) – Friendship. I have signed Friendship but I don't know you and you don't know me … TAKE A GOOD TIP. DON'T BE ON PREMISES MAY 13-15 OR MAY 20 -15 [sic].

'Letter to Charles Hohenrein', May 1915

A second letter arrived later that day:

Dear Sir, I hope you got my last letter and I hope you have taken notice of it as your shop is going to be broken up … I dare not let you know too much as I would be found and I would have to suffer. The reason I have taken such an interest in warning you is because when I was a boy your parents and those who kept your shop were very good to me and many a time when I was hungry and needed bread so you see I wish you no harm in any way. Your shop is not the only shop but there are others and I am warning you and I shall have to carry out my work when I am ordered by my chief the Captain. Sir, if you will put a letter in the *Daily Mail* I will know you have got my letter. I do not mean a bold one but one of a mild kind. The reason for it is to avenge LUSITANIA – Friendship – 2.

Around midnight, a group of youths duly attacked Hohenrein's shop but were identified and arrested. Having served in the East Riding Yeomanry and taken out naturalisation, Hohenrein offered a reward of £500 (equivalent to over £30,000 in 2014) to anyone who could prove he wasn't British. There were no takers, but a letter had to be provided by the Chief Constable:

The bearer, Mr C. H. Hohenrein, is a British born subject whom I have known since his youth. He is a man of the highest integrity and honour and I have the most implicit confidence and reliance in him. He is well known to most of the leading citizens in this district.

Like the Schonhuts, the Hohenrein family also had relatives in the Ruhleben internment camp:

There seem to be quite a number of prisoners interned here who complain that, on account of their possessing German names, their wives and children in England have been subject to violence and outrages. This I cannot believe, this is entirely un-English and until I have more definite news upon the subject shall very much doubt its accuracy. Besides, what is a name? Merely a legacy inherited from our ancestors and in our case one of which we may be justly proud. But at any rate this would be impossible to happen to us. Our services in the interests of the British public will not be easily forgotten and our loyal sentiments no-one can doubt.

George Hohenrein, 'Letter to Hull from
German Internment Camp'

Charles, however, took a different view of what a name meant. In November 1915, Hohenrein's shop was no more. As Charles Ross, he received no more threats.

In France, attacks at Loos and Neuve Chapelle had been costly failures, as both sides struggled to adapt to trench fighting. The stalemate on the Western Front was unbroken and so, for a time, attention turned elsewhere.

At the beginning of the twentieth century, the Ottoman Empire based in Constantinople (modern day Istanbul) was regarded as 'the sick man of Europe', weakened by political instability, military defeat and civil strife following a century of decline. In 1908, a group of young officers, known as the 'Young Turks', had seized power and installed Mehmed IV as Sultan. Britain, France, Germany and Russia all courted the new regime, seeking to influence the country's leadership as the Ottoman Empire's geographic position meant that her neutrality in the event of war in Europe was of significant interest to Russia, and her French and British allies.

As the crisis in Europe deepened, Ottoman leaders reached an agreement with Germany against Russia and the commandeering of two Ottoman battleships under construction in Britain served to undermine pro-British politicians in Constantinople. Immediately, the Germans offered two of their ships to the Ottoman Navy as replacements and sailed them up the Dardanelles Straits in breach of international law. In September 1914, command of the Ottoman navy was taken over by Rear Admiral Souchon of the Imperial German Navy who, acting without the agreement of the Ottoman government, ordered the Dardanelles closed. The two ships provided by the Germans sailed into the Black Sea and shelled Russian ports and on 2 November, the Russians declared war on the Ottomans, to be followed a few days later by Britain and France. Fighting broke out in Mesopotamia as the British attempted to seize Ottoman controlled oilfields, and the Ottomans in turn prepared to attack British interests in Egypt.

In 1915, First Sea Lord Winston Churchill proposed using obsolete British ships in an attack on the Dardanelles to force a passage for supplies to Russia, threaten Constantinople itself, and hopefully draw in the former Ottoman possessions of Greece and Bulgaria into the war on the allied side. It would also provide a response to Grand Duke Nicholas' request for help to relieve pressure on his forces in the Caucasus region, where Ottoman troops were pressing home their offensive. Since the Russian front was tying down large numbers of German troops who might otherwise have been in France, it was vital to support Russia and so an operation was planned to land British and French troops on the Gallipoli peninsula and from there to advance towards Constantinople.

On 25 April 1915, the first troops landed and began to push inland, but the attack went disastrously wrong. After only a few miles, they were halted by a far stronger force of defenders than had been anticipated and the allies began to dig in. By June it was clear that more forces would be needed to break out of the beachhead positions, but it was also clear

Suvla Bay. The Yorkshire landing.

that the areas under allied control were too small to accommodate more landings. A new plan was developed to land troops to the north, at Suvla Bay, and to then link up with the Australians and New Zealanders of the ANZAC Corps. Chosen to take part in the landings, due to take place in August, were the Yorkshiremen of 32 Brigade of the 11th (Northern) Division.

We knew that the four hundred men of the East Yorks were mostly fresh from training and few had seen action, so every sailor was given two soldiers to look after. We gave them our hammocks, made sure they ate well and gave them our rum. You see, we knew that where they were going would be like Hell on earth, so we gave them all the love we could, because they were going to need it. There was all these feelings. That's why I admire the British, they take it and they're quiet.

As we approached Suvla Bay on the night of 6–7 August, it was the darkness before the dawn. I stood on the gangway which had been fitted over the stern to allow the troops to walk down into the motor lighters. As the soldiers followed each other down with their rifles one got hit by a sniper and screamed out. I told him to shut up and put up with the pain or he would frighten the rest – that was my first scream of war ... I did my best to cheer them up and encourage them. But most of the time, I was quiet because there wasn't much you could say in the face of all that horror. It was important that they had their own thoughts, they had to come to terms with it in their own way.

Ordinary Seaman Jack Gearing,
Benbow Battalion, Royal Naval Division.

We were taken up in Destroyers, or rather on Destroyers, as the men were packed like herrings on deck. We passed fairly close to Cape Helles end of Gallipoli, and could see all that was happening around Achi Baba. The run took 3½ hours. We landed in the new type of lighter, which has a little bridge that lets down at the bow, worked by chains. They draw exceedingly little and ground very easily on the beach. I am not certain in how many they are meant to hold, but we packed three double Companies on one when we eventually moved to Gallipoli ... Company commanders were told that the move was coming that day. We had the usual parade at 5.45 am. There was an officer's conference at 2.00 and maps were supplied us of Suvla Bay district, and the Colonel issued orders for the battalion's section. A, B & C. C[ompanies], under Major Roberts ... were to land at the beach south of the Salt Lake, proceed up the beach about 200 yards, and form line with flank platoons in fours, then wheel half left, which would bring us north east and attack the hill Lala Baba. The orders were, no loading, bayonet only

… We marched out at quarter to four, and we loaded on two lighters which were towed by destroyers, the destroyers also being packed with troops. We were towed from the bow of the destroyer, steering ourselves. The lighter too has a little engine of its own which can do about six miles an hour. It was an exceedingly dark night, almost pitch black. As we neared the peninsula we travelled slower and slower, creeping along eventually. There were searchlights moving from the direction Achi Baba, two of them seemed to pick us up. We had been told by the Colonel that the Brigade was covering the landings, and the 6th Yorkshire was covering the Brigade, so that the Yorkshire Brigade in that respect had been honoured by selection. As we neared the shore under our own engines we were greeted with a burst of rifle fire … On arriving at the base of Lala Baba I ordered a charge and ran up the hill. About three quarters of the way up we came upon a Turkish trench, very narrow and flush with the ground. We ran over this, and they fired into our rear, firing going on at this time from several directions. I shouted out that the Yorkshire Regiment was coming in order to avoid running into our own people. We ran on, and about twelve paces further on, so far as I can judge, came to another trench, which we also crossed. We were again fired into from the rear. I ordered the Company to jump back into the second trench and we got into this, which was so narrow that wherever you were you had to stop, it being quite impossible for one man to pass another, or even to walk up it, unless you moved sideways. Another difficulty was that if there were any wounded or dead men in the bottom of the trench it was impossible to avoid treading on them in passing. There was a little communication trench running from right to left behind me, and whenever I shouted an order, a Turk, who appeared to be in this trench, fired at me from a distance apparently five or ten yards. One of our men on my left was sitting on a prisoner, and there were four wounded or dead men just in the bottom of the trench near me. I chucked out several Turkish rifles, in case Turks were shamming, and took a clip from of them, which I brought home as my sole trophy. I had some difficulty in getting anybody to fire down the communication trench in order to quiet the enterprising Turk who was endeavouring to pot me with great regularity, but eventually got him. We had at this time not picked up any of the remainder of the battalion, so far as I could ascertain. I therefore ordered another charge over the crest of the hill which was just in front of us. We ran on, shouting that the Yorkshires were coming … I was hit by soft lead round bullet smashing the upper part of my left arm completely. I got one of the men there – Private J. Cole, 11873 Y. Company 8th Duke of Wellington's Regiment to put on my field dressing, and made him fix up a tourniquet with the handle of his entrenching instrument … There were no stretchers or ambulances working at this time, which was somewhere about 6 a.m. on Saturday morning, so I thought I would make a push to get down to the beach before my strength went. I started to walk in with my right arm round his shoulders, he holding my left hand and the handle of the entrenching instrument ... Six hours in a dressing station, absolutely unsheltered from sun or shrapnel, where the medical officer of the Northumberland Fusiliers, tied me up very successfully & a stretcher journey of about 3½ hours in the afternoon, 2½ hours in a row-boat on a stretcher, where I got wet to the akin in a tropical rainstorm, which left me a legacy of five inches of water in the stretcher, and arriving just too late to get on to the 'Soudan' Hospital Ship, a further journey to the *Valdavia* brought me at about 6.45 p.m. on deck, where I arrived with a very healthy attack of ague amongst other ills.

And that is all I know personally about the attack of Lala Baba and the battle of Suvla Bay, both of which cost the 6th Battalion of the Yorkshire Regiment very heavily indeed, our only consolation being that we carried out the most difficult task assigned to us, unaided, and have not let down the reputation gained by the regiment gained in France.

Major W. Boyd Shannon, 6th Yorkshire Regiment.

The Yorkshire landing was chaotic even by the confused standards of the Gallipoli campaign. The maps issued were poor quality and in the darkness men became lost. Soon, the Yorkshiremen of 32 Brigade were scattered across a wide area, each battalion fighting its own battle. On 8 August, after three days of fighting, the exhausted men of the 6th East Yorkshires moved into action again.

The rampart of hills to the east of us was black against the chill, pale sky as we moved out across the grey flats that led to the foot of Tekke Tepe, towering up to nearly 1,000 feet ahead of us. And we came under fire from our right flank almost from the very start. The foot-hills of the range were rough with boulders, and deep cut by rocky ravines. As we moved on and on, up and up, men got lost in the prickly scrub oak, 'holly', they called it, and it became increasingly difficult to maintain any sort of formation. But the enemy's fire grew in volume as we mounted, poured into us at ever decreasing range from the right and from the front ... Those who were hit stayed where they fell, and those who were whole climbed on. The only complaint heard upon that hillside was that no enemy could be seen to fire upon ... About thirty of us reached the top of the hill, perhaps a few more. And when there were about twenty left we turned and went down again. We had reached the highest point and the furthest point that British forces from Suvla Bay were destined to reach. But we naturally knew nothing of that.

Lieutenant John Still, 6th East Yorkshires

The attacking units had suffered heavily and needed reinforcements. Ernest Lye had missed the initial attack due to illness. He caught up with his mates on the 9th:

We could see them in the distance, skirting the Salt Lake and, even though we were so far away, they appeared to be almost too tired to drag one foot after another. It was when we came up with them and could see their faces that we got the biggest shock of our lives. What terrible thing had put that indescribable look of horror in their eyes? They looked haunted with a memory of the sight of hell! With their faces dirty and unkempt, and with their clothes torn and ragged, I thought of them four days ago as they passed me as I stood by the doctor's tent, with their laughing faces and tin triangles. I looked for some of the familiar faces – Ernie Shaw, yes! He's there. Tommy Knott, no. Where's Tommy Knott? 'Killed.' 'Herbert Butterworth, and his pal Frank Boyes; have you seen them?' 'Frank was wounded and Butterworth went back to help him, and we haven't seen them since'. Where's Paddy Whitehouse? 'Oh! Over there with Lance Corporal Hullah' and so on. There were twenty left of our platoon of sixty-one. Only two officers left in the whole battalion ... We had a roll call on the slope of York Hill [Lala Baba] and the sight will be pictured forever in my mind. I thought of a picture I had once seen, giving a similar incident in the

Edmund Yerbury Priestman, 1890–1915.

Crimean War. The picture was good but the artist couldn't put into the picture the wild haunted look I saw in the eyes of my comrades as they answered their names, nor could he put on canvas the heart broken sobs as some man's name was called and not answered.

Private Ernest Lye, 8th Duke of Wellington's Regiment.

Like the battle further south, the landings at Suvla Bay settled down into a routine of trench warfare in the blistering heat, interspersed with attacks by both sides:

You must try and imagine us … squatting on our haunches in a shallow and dusty trench, listening to the most appalling uproar you could dream of. Behind us our big guns are roaring, above us the shells are tearing through the air, and in front of us, all up the long valley ahead, the crash of their bursting is simply deafening. Somewhere (all too vaguely described to us) are three lines of Turkish trenches which must be taken to-day. But the valley is broad and thick with bushes, and the enemy is cunning to conceal his position. No matter! This terrific bombardment will surely overawe him and make our advance a simple matter. So we sit and listen and wait for the hour to come when we are due to hurl line after line of British Tommies against those trenches.

Can you picture the feelings of all of us as we watch the minute-hand slowly creep towards three? Ten minutes only now. Now only seven.

And what of us all when that hand shall have touched the half-hour?

The dentist's grisly waiting-den, the ante-room to the operating theatre – these multiplied a thousand-fold in their dread anticipation.

And now the moment has come. A whistle sounds – a scramble over the trusty parapet we have learned to know as a shield for so many hours, and the valley is before us. 'Whiss! whissss!' The air is full on every side with invisible death, 'Whisss! phutt!' A bullet kicks up a little spray of dust from the dry grey earth underfoot, another and another to left and right. The sensation of terror is swallowed in an overwhelming conviction that the only possible course is forward – forward at any cost. That is what we have been telling ourselves all through the long waiting, and that is our only clear impression now. Forward – and we instinctively bend as one does to meet a hailstorm, and rush for it.

Lieutenant Edmund Yerbury Priestman,
6th York and Lancaster

At 11 o'clock the Captain told us we had to attack the Turks, and he said, when we were about to jump out of the trench, 'Give them socks, lads,' but we had no sooner got our heads out of the top of the trench than there came a perfect hail of bullets and some of our poor lads never got on the top before they were shot dead. But I advanced with the lot, and we kept lying down as we advanced, and as I lay behind some cover, the boys kept falling on either side of me, and the bullets were flying over my head and past my side. It was hell upon earth, and I am sure they never experienced anything like it in France. I wonder how I got through, for I was advancing on the left when a shell burst that sent me over the cliff with a drop of sixty feet.

Private Arthur Howorth, Todmorden

At noon the order came along to get ready for an advance. Then we started, I Company leading. We had just got nicely going when 'ping, ping,' the, Turks had us. Then we got it, we dropped like rain – so did the bullets and shrapnel. About the third rush, I was on my stomach, taking cover as best I could, when, a bullet entered my shoulder and travelled down my back, where it now is. For hours I lay there and could not move. I managed at last to crawl away down a gully to a doctor who bandaged me up and sent me down to the shore.

Private Philip Sutcliffe

Trench life, Gallipoli.

Unable to break out of the beachhead, the men dug in. Throughout the long siege that lay ahead, men found time to socialise:

It is a matter of extreme satisfaction to all of us connected with the *Herald* to know that our paper is serving useful and novel purposes in the interests of you boys at the Front. Here is a case in point. Private L Nightingale, of Pannal Junction, landed in Suvla Bay (Dardenelles). He was not aware of the presence in that part of any Harrogate boys. You may imagine his delight when he received a certain copy of the Herald to find that Harrogate soldiers were very near him. He ascertained this from the picture page and accompanying soldiers' letters. At the first opportunity he made a tour of the trenches, and by the help of the Herald portraits not only found friends but Harrogate men he did not know, identifying them by their likenesses. You can imagine the lonely feelings he first entertained, surrounded by so many strange faces, was soon dispelled. Spofforth people will be pleased to know that he found Myers, of Spofforth, an old Sunday school fellow. Nightingale served three years with Mr Gunter at Wetherby as a jockey. Nightingale had to go into hospital at Malta, but is now doing well.

W. H. Breare, *Harrogate Herald*, 1 December 1915

Nearby, Edmund Priestman, former Scoutmaster to the 16 Sheffield Boy Scouts wrote letters to his family and his former scout pack describing life at the front:

AFTERNOON TEA

Gallipoli Peninsula. Of course, being the celebrated Yorkshire landing, Suvla is much better run than anywhere else! And even here things aren't too good. This is not the Suvla it was in August; what with mules and stores and the other modern conveniences they have planted here there might not be a war on at all. The trenches themselves are getting monotonous, too, and you have to walk about half a mile from here to get any real excitement. We do sometimes get shelled where my dug-out is, but on top of the hill they get it every day. I went paying calls the other day, and the man I went to call on said: 'You'd better come inside, the shells are due about now.' Well, he'd hardly spoken before a big shrapnel came along-whizz!

We both dived inside his dug-out and he lay on top of me (me being the visitor – there's etiquette in these things), and so escaped being hit. The next that came along blew about four sandbags on to us, and my pal remarked: 'They'll really start in a minute!' Well, I was simply quivering with emotion as it was. Anyway, we put the sandbags back, and the next shell dropped slap into a group of fellows about ten yards away, blowing all the money out of one man's pocket and part of him along with it – horrid splash. The other man, an officer of one of the regiments in our brigade, simply vanished in a cloud of dust and we only found unimportant parts of him when we came to have a look round. Regular jig-saw puzzle he was, so we finally gave it up. By this time I was quite abject in my terror, and when they told me that a Taube [enemy aircraft] was coming over I simply set off and ran like a rabbit down that hill. It turned out to be one of our own machines, and they caught me and brought me back to have a cup of tea with them. Owing to the shelling, they said, their tea-parties were losing popularity and they weren't going to miss a visitor when he did come. But I didn't make what you would call a really good [guest].

Lieutenant Edmund Yerbury Priestman,
6th York and Lancaster

A thrilling account has come to hand of a gallant stand made recently at Suvla Bay by a party of the 6th (Service) battalion York and Lancaster Regiment, under the command of Second-Lieutenant E. Y. Priestman. This will be of interest locally, as a very large percentage of the recruits raised for this Battalion were residents of Sheffield and district. Lieutenant Priestman was a Sheffield scoutmaster. The account says:

Our trenches ran along the coast, near Jeffson's Post, and orders had been received for us to work along the furthermost sap to enable us to gain a portion of higher ground on the left of our sap. In order to do this it was necessary to leave our trenches at night, run forward with sandbags to the place marked, and dig in as rapidly as possible. On this particular night, Lieutenant Priestman and about thirty N. C. O. s and men were detailed to make good this position.

Leaving the trenches about 1.00 a.m., they gained the position without incident, and commenced to entrench as quietly as possible. 'Shortly afterwards the Turks rushed the position. Lieutenant Priestman did not retire, but opened a rapid fire, which kept the enemy at bay for a while, but, coming on again with a combined rush, they decimated the whole of the gallant little band.' Lieutenant Priestman fell, fighting till the last, and Regimental Sergeant Warr was also killed while taking up a message to him. 'We attacked the position again in larger force next night, and succeeded in holding it. The bodies of Lieutenant Priestman and several men were discovered, all the wounded having been removed by the enemy'. The captured position was named 'Priestman's Post' by Headquarters, to commemorate the gallantry of this young officer, who was respected by all who knew him.

Sheffield Daily Telegraph, 5 February 1916

On 25 April 1915, the SS *River Clyde* was deliberately run ashore on 'V' beach to land troops of the Dublin Fusiliers. Also among the troops aboard were men of the 1/1st West Riding Engineers.

By 20 December 1915, the survivors of the Yorkshire landing had been withdrawn from Gallipoli and the last men left by January 1916. The operation had been a total and costly failure. As the last men left Anzac Cove, one was seen to nod towards one of the many makeshift cemeteries lining the shore and say quietly, 'I hope they don't hear us marching away'.

As 32 Brigade prepared to leave Gallipoli, back in England, the Leeds, Bradford, Barnsley, Sheffield and Hull Pals had all been grouped into a new formation – the 31st Division. Having finally managed to complete effective training, in late November the Division received a warning order to prepare to sail for France. Advance parties began to depart but on 2 December new orders were received that the Division would instead be sent to Egypt to reinforce the garrison there.

I remember leaving Barnsley, Barnsley went mad that night. They lined the streets all the way through. Everybody was kissing everybody else. I'll never forget that.

Private Harry Hall, Barnsley Pals

We didn't know where we were being sent, but they did issue us with sunhats.

Private Charlie Swales, Barnsley Pals

It would not be a pleasure cruise:

I really can hardly bear to think of the hardships [the men] are bound to go through during this voyage. They are packed absolutely like sardines right away below where on ordinary occasions, cargo and steerage are.

Lieutenant Morris Bickersteth, Bradford Pals

The furthest I'd been prior to that trip was Cleethorpes, maybe Blackpool. I was as sick as a dog. I lay on the top deck for three days, I daren't go down to eat. I remember the first day I went down, I got to the top of the gangway steps going down and I met this fellow with a trayful of Quaker Oats. When I saw that tray of Quaker Oats, that was enough. I went back.

Private Harry Hall, Barnsley Pals

Leeds Pals on their way to Egypt 1915. At the centre is Pte Jogendra Sen, an Indian student at Leeds University.

We lost three men, didn't find them for five days because they were sick ... We passed Gibraltar and all of a sudden 'Becky' [Private John Beckton] appeared. You never saw a walking corpse in all your life. He'd had nothing to eat and he said 'I don't want nothing to drink!' He could hardly talk ... We had rations for fifteen men, six of us ... . I was only sick once, two or three minutes and I just got it off my chest ... of course they said if you are sick go down amongst the horses, the mules, and talk to them, they'll do you good, but the stench of them made it worse too!

Private Clifford Hollingworth, Leeds Pals

There was me and 'Hoppy' hanging over the side and an old deck hand came up to us and says, 'Now boys you can spew and spew to your heart's content, but if you feel a ring in your mouth swallow hard cos its your arsehole.'

Private Frank Lindley, Barnsley Pals

After floundering around the Bay of Biscay for days, the ships finally passed Gibraltar and soon reached the naval base at Malta. About three o'clock in the afternoon we sighted Gozo Island and, about an hour later, Malta. The first sight was absolutely magnificent. The first thing we noticed was the tents of the soldiers garrisoned there. The towers and castle-like structures with their coloured domes were shining in the sun. As soon as we got in the harbor mouth, we were surrounded by the Maltese boys in their little boats crying out for silver coins. If you drop them in the water near their boats, they dive in and catch them two or three feet below the surface. I was surprised to see the number of cruisers and battleships there were in the harbor, not to mention submarines, destroyers and innumerable steamers and motor boats ... We couldn't go ashore, so I didn't see much of the town. My only regret was that I did not get some lace for Florence and her sisters.

Sergeant Harold Saville, Bradford Pals

A few days later, the convoy arrived in Egypt:

When the boat stopped at Port Said some of the natives were coming on row boats. They wore fezes and they had like a long smock on down to their ankles. One of the lads said 'Are they lads or lasses?' Suddenly one of the lads had a bright idea. 'There's only one way to find art', he said, 'tipple the bugger upside darn', so one was upended to see if it were a lad or a lass, it was a lad! It was all in fun, they were just typical collier lads.

Private Charlie Swales, Barnsley Pals

Port Said is a strange place. The houses are all on the 'flats' system. They have straight roofs and from a distance of 200 or 300 yards it looks like a pile of all finished buildings as though a half built and then left. The lower classes keep goats and hens and pigs inside the houses. There are people of all races here, Arabs, Egyptians French and many different coloured races and from this fact naturally there are scores of types of dressing. Most of the inhabitants are very scantily clothed in dresses of gorgeous colours. In the streets men and boys pester you in droves hawking smallwares, cigarettes, oranges etc. All over the place are drinking saloons; high class with an orchestra under a veranda and lounges outside and very low class affairs. Nearly all shopkeepers speak English and many of them 7–10 languages.

Private Fred Conquest, Bradford Pals

We visited the city streets in the evenings. We were warned to go out with two or three others, side arms [bayonets] to be worn and not to visit Arab Quarters where the loose women were. There were many strange sights in the streets, conjurors, bird trainers, tumblers, all these performing on their own little carpets for a stage, and the trinket or fruit sellers with their trays in front of them. Also the money changers. These all formed a challenge to the rough lads from White Abbey, Bradford. One would be arguing the price of something, then with about a dozen pals gathered round, up would go the tray and all the boys would grab anything that came their way and off like lightning before the screaming Arab could complain to the military police ... One afternoon later, I was having a swim near the canal entrance, where many creek-like shallows were to be found. A small rowing boat was coming my way and as it smoothly passed by I saw to my horror it contained a dead soldier with his tongue almost cut out and hanging out of his mouth. He had been found in the Arab Quarter! I was almost sick at the sight.

Private Sam B. Wood, Bradford Pals

The sand where we are encamped is full of ants and sand lice. We are getting lousy by now, but it does not matter. I am as happy as a mud lark. The only thing that bothers me is that I haven't got a penny.

Sergeant Harold Saville, Bradford Pals

After a few days we received our pay, 3s 6d. No back pay as yet, but we felt rich, really rich. It was a great joy to supplement the rations at 7. 00 on the morning. An enterprising Arab had set up a small brazier at the end of the lines on which he cooked the small Egyptian eggs, and one could get a small teacake with a fried egg on it for a penny ha'penny. We had hoped for a decent Christmas Dinner, but unfortunately on that day the biscuits provided were green mouldy and unfit to eat. We had to fill up with bully beef.

Private Sam B. Wood, Bradford Pals

Saturday 25 December. Fine sunny day which makes it difficult to realize it is Xmas. 4pm. About 500 Non-Conformists had dinner at the Casino Palace Hotel, a first class place. We were charged 2*s* 6*d* and had turkey and plum pudding which certainly made it feel more 'Christmassy' than anything although we did not get big portions as we do at home.

Boxing Day. Two soldiers drowned while bathing. One soldier (KOYLI) found dead on sands. Believed to have been drunk and murdered by Arabs. We are not allowed to go in what is called the Arab Town which is a terrible place of vice and treachery, but the fellows slip in and have a lively time. The shops are open on Sundays as usual, the Sabbath is scarcely regarded here.

29 December. A soldier of the E. Yorks died from cruel treatment of Arabs.

Diary, Private Fred Conquest, Bradford Pals

After three months, rumours began to spread.

We had a 'whiff' we were moving. We rumbled it on the bush telegraph. It was surprising how news got around. You got to know things you didn't read about. It just seemed to filter through. Some said India but it wasn't India, it was the other way. It was France. We got to know that at Verdun the French were getting a smacking.

Private Frank Lindley, Barnsley Pals

Early on the morning of 8 March 1916, the Barnsley and Sheffield Pals set out for Port Said. A very different war was awaiting them.

4

1916: 'WHEN THE BARRAGE LIFTS'

After the initial panic at the outbreak of war, business had quickly picked up, especially in the mill towns of the West Riding, who were soon operating at full capacity to turn out uniforms, weapons and ammunition.

Only the clothing operatives were greatly perturbed. There were fears that the industry – of such vital importance to Leeds – might not recover from the emphatic check of war. It's 'good time', however, was not long in coming. Army orders soon gave ample employment. Contracts for boots, and for khaki cloth, too, rolled in. The early queues of workless grew smaller and smaller. Trade prospects all round brightened, though it meant a diversion of ways and means and some considerable adaptation to the novelty of the industrial situation.

William Herbert Scott

The future of the cotton trade aroused considerable anxiety for a time, and it was curious how far out in their reckoning most of the prophets were in this respect. The general opinion was that trade would be paralysed, leading to a period of great privation; but these fears were soon found to be without foundation. Work was more abundant, and wages higher, in most trades, than ever before, due partly to the scarcity of labour, but more particularly to the grant of increased wages to meet the higher cost of living. In anticipation of the expected hard times, Relief Committees were appointed and Relief Funds opened, and a movement was organised for the feeding of necessitous School children. This latter movement grew to such dimensions that for the week ending 25 September the number of children being supplied with free meals was 560; but by the following January conditions had so far altered that the number of so-called necessitous children on the books had fallen to eleven.

John A. Lee

Let there be no bunkum about patriotism. The employers have a one sided view of patriotism: that it is no concern of theirs but that it is part of the employees' contract … In the factory districts patriotism is what operatives practice and what the employers get paid for.

The Worker, 2 January 1915

Recruiting figures around the country had varied considerably. In Leeds, it was estimated that only 5.2 per cent of men eligible for military service had actually volunteered and in Bradford only 4 per cent. Nowhere in the country had more than a quarter of the men eligible to enlist done so, and in Yorkshire, as a whole, the figure was just 17 per cent. In response, the War Office sent Londoner John Hunter Watts, a prominent member of the socialist movement's old guard, north to try to encourage workers to enlist. As *The Worker* reported on 18 September 1915, he had asked to pay particular attention to Huddersfield since, as he told a meeting there, 'the War Office informed him that the most serious opposition to recruiting came from this district'.

He said that the places where he considered effort was most needed were towns where there was a certain amount of hostility to recruiting. Huddersfield and Halifax ran one another very close in that respect. Without doubt, in the West Riding there existed a strong element for which he could find no better word than anti-socialist pacifism.

The Worker, 23 October 1915.

By late 1915,

The average recruiting speech became a mixture of abuse, cajolery and threats … the men secured by pressure of this kind could hardly be described as volunteers … the whole business has become manifestly unfair … men were induced to join whose business and family obligations ought to have secured them a respite, while insensitive people with no such responsibilities smiled and sat tight.

H. Cartmell

Anti-conscription rally.

Millions of men had already volunteered, but if the British Army was to expand to the seventy divisions Lord Kitchener had said were needed, it was increasingly obvious that some form of compulsion would be needed. In some areas, such as Huddersfield, the local Poor Law Guardians had taken the decision to withdraw any support to military age men, in effect leaving them no alternative but to enlist or starve. It led to one opponent asking whether this was because it was felt 'better to shoot them away, than to shoot them at home'. Conscription had been a political issue for almost a century and calls for European-style National Service had been rising over the past two decades, although they were matched by equally strident opposition.

[We] oppose conscription as a violation of principles and a menace to the liberty of the people and pledge [ourselves] to support any members of Socialist Sunday Schools who are prepared to resist, whatever the consequences.

'Yorkshire Union of Socialist Sunday Schools Minutes',
27 November 1915

With feelings against conscription so strong, a compromise was suggested. After being appointed Director of Recruiting in October 1915, Lord Derby proposed what would become known as 'the Derby Scheme':

men of military age would come forward and attest their willingness to serve when called up in age groups, as they were in France and Germany, but would then be free to return home until such time as the call came. Class 1 would be single men born in 1875, Class 2 in 1876 and so on up to Class 23, born in 1897. Class 24 would include married men born in 1875 and carry on to Class 46, married men born in 1897. The widely held assumption was that married men would not be called up before single men.

In order to make the scheme effective, National Registration had taken place to identify who was available to do what. Every person was required to provide details of age, address and occupation. Those men whose skills were deemed to be vital to the war effort had their cards marked with a star to signify that they were in a reserved occupation. Every other male aged between eighteen and forty-one would be liable for conscription.

Knowing that compulsory service was on its way, many chose to attest under the Derby Scheme, with Hull producing 12,000 men in just three days. Unfortunately, it was soon discovered that although married men had come forward, only 343,000 of the million or so unmarried men had done so. By the time those men had been sifted and exemptions claimed, the Derby Scheme contributed just 43,000 men to the Army. Some wondered whether the scheme had been allowed to fail to strengthen the argument in favour of conscription.

[I feel] somewhat in a position of a receiver who was put in to wind up a bankrupt concern.

Lord Derby, quoted in *The Star*, 6 October 1915

Even before the scheme had failed, legislation was being passed to introduce the first Military Service Act on 27 January 1916, which brought in compulsory military service for all males who 'on 15 August 1915 was ordinarily resident in Great Britain and who had attained the age of nineteen but was not yet forty-one and on 2 November 1915 was unmarried or a widower without dependent children'. Under the terms of the 'Bachelor's Bill', as it became known, unless he met certain exceptions or had reached the age of forty-one before the appointed date, from 2 March 1916 every unmarried male citizen was deemed to have enlisted for general service with the colours and was, for the time being, regarded as being in the Army reserve. Those with a preference for service in the Navy could state it, and would be offered to the Admiralty. Under the draconian Defence of the Realm Act, mothers

Leeds Pals digging in in the Egyptian desert.

who tried to 'harbour' their sons in an attempt to escape service would themselves be arrested and have their boys taken anyway.

To ensure that men answered the call, police and soldiers began a process of 'round ups' in which railway stations, cinemas, football grounds and other places where military age men might be found were targeted for raids. Any men found were required to produce their papers, or face arrest. In one round up in Keighley, 150 men were arrested at a performance of *Little Marie* – a 'two act drama of the slums' – at the Cosy Corner Picture House, but most turned out to be exempted munitions workers. Until people got used to carrying their papers with them at all times, these events were always followed by streams of anxious relatives arriving at the police stations with the required documentation to secure their release. Elsewhere, in industry, a process known as 'combing out' began to identify those men whose jobs were either not vital to the war effort or could be done by someone else. Major J. R. P. Newman, the MP For Enfield, reported in October 1916 that in one factory alone, 550 of the 650 military aged men working there were single.

Men not in uniform came to be regarded as 'shirkers' and in some places feelings ran high against them. In order to balance universal conscription with the demands for skilled workers to maintain the war effort, the willingness of unions to strike in order to protect their members from call up and those who claimed moral and religious opposition to service, a network of around 2,000 tribunals were set up around the country, presided over by local representatives from various walks of life, – described by one historian as being the 'sort of people you'd get to sign your passport application'. Their job was to hear appeals for exemption from call up in cases where service would cause a family particular hardship, gravely damage businesses, take away a worker with particular skills from important war work and, most difficult of all, from those asking for exemption on the grounds of pacifist conscience.

The tribunals worked hard. In Huddersfield, there were almost 19,000 applications in 1916 alone. The Leeds Tribunal sat 435 times during the war to hear 55,000 appeals relating to 27,000 individuals. In the first year of conscription, almost 750,000 claimed exemptions of one kind or another, a figure only slightly lower than the 770,000 who answered their call up. Despite their reputation today, figures show that on the whole, the tribunals appear to have been sympathetic to genuine cases, with 75 per cent of applicants given exemptions ranging from a couple of months to absolute exemptions protecting them for the rest of the war. However, the definition of 'genuine' hardship was often tested to the limit. The Keighley Tribunal heard from a man who felt he was indispensible at home as the only man in the village able to cut hair. Tripe dressers, corset makers and ladies outfitters all tried to convince tribunals that their work was vital to the war effort with varying degrees of success while tribunal members expressed concern about the number of relatives who seemed to suddenly need care. 'Senile decay sets in at a very early age [around here],' noted one chairman.

As the need for manpower became more pressing, the standards expected of recruits plummeted. Men who were rejected as unfit for the Army in 1914 found themselves classified as 'A1' for frontline service in 1916. It led to some bizarre stories:

Applicant: I have a conscientious objection.
The Chairman: I think you have more than a conscientious objection. You have an objection on material grounds.
Applicant: Well, I wish to go on with the conscientious objection.
The Chairman: It is no use wasting the time of the court. There must be an exemption.
The Military Representative: On what grounds?
Applicant: Conscientious grounds.
The Chairman: On the ground that he only has one leg.

Sir William Stephens: We have a conscientious objection to calling up a man
who only has one leg.

'Report of the Salford Tribunal' reported in the
York Herald, 5 April 1916

The same paper also reported:

At the Hertford tribunal, a coachman applied for exemption because he had
only one eye. When asked for evidence of this he dropped his right eye into his
hand. The court allowed the claim.

Lots of you Harrogate boys will know that bright-eyed little chap who looks
after the lavatories in the gardens on Prospect Hill. You have often seen him in
the streets forging ahead with his crutch and stick, therefore you know that he
has lost his leg. As I was going to Court on Friday morning he stopped me, with
an unusually animated smile. He said: 'If you don't see me again you'll know I'm
in the Army.' At which I smiled. He then told me he had been to York the day
before, and, though it was obvious that he had but one leg (for he has not an
artificial limb), the farce of a medical examination was gone through. Oh, yes,
lots of little things like that happen when all the previously rejected are bound
to come up for re-examination. My genial friend did not seem a bit put out. He
regarded it as a huge joke. I fancy I see you boys smiling as you read about it.

W. H. Breare, *Harrogate Herald*, 13 June 1917

Of the thousands of applications heard, only a small proportion were on
the grounds of conscientious objection – in Huddersfield, described as 'a
hotbed of pacifism', only 111 (0. 8 per cent) of the 19,000 applications
were made by 'Conchies'. For people like Mrs Philipson of Worsbrough
Bridge, who had five sons and two grandsons, already in the Army, or
Eliza Moxon of nearby Racecommon Road, Barnsley, with six sons and
a son-in-law serving, sympathy with those who chose to stay at home
was in short supply.

If I had my way I would send the whole lot of them ... to fix barbed wire and
sandbags to protect our dear Tommies at the front.

Walter Blakey, letter to the *Harrogate Herald*

Those whose religious, moral or political beliefs objected to military service
often accepted roles in the Medical Corps or in supply line posts. Others
went to a specially created 'Non-Combatant Corps', including 'Agricultural
Companies' run by the military and providing labour on farms and for
forestry work in Britain. Some Quakers had already volunteered for the
Friends Ambulance Unit and had provided valuable help for the wounded,

Conscientious objectors were widely condemned for hiding behind the freedoms being upheld by the efforts of soldiers at the front.

gaining the respect of the men at the front. Given the city's close links with the Society of Friends, York Tribunal dealt with many applicants claiming to be Quakers, including that of Robert Bilton, a stationer who 'had belonged to the Society of Friends since the outbreak of war and the Vegetarian Society since 1904', who argued that as a vegetarian he could not shed blood and refused to serve in either a medical capacity or behind the front in the supply lines.

Such men were harder to deal with. Those with objections to killing could be offered non-combatant roles, but a small core of men, known as 'absolutists', refused any compromise, claiming that any work they were directed to do would contribute to the war effort. For some, such men were heroes willing to suffer and even die rather than to compromise their beliefs. For others, they were deluded cranks who believed that the laws that applied to everyone else should not apply to them and who relished the opportunity to be seen as martyrs. Military service was a legal requirement for all men deemed suitable to serve. The tribunals heard from applicants who, for whatever reason, felt they should be exempted and were frequently sympathetic to individual circumstances. However, there were some whose sole argument, to the tribunal at least, seemed to be that they didn't want to join the Army and that this should be reason enough. The problem was how to deal with such men. If they were allowed to flout the law, then the whole system would collapse.

In his application, Arthur Gardiner of Huddersfield said he was twenty-six-years of age, was employed as a wool and cotton dyer and could not conscientiously undertake combatant or non-combatant military service. For a number of years he had devoted his time and energy, both publicly and privately, to the economic and moral upliftment of humanity. He was opposed to all forms of militarism, believing it to be 'detrimental to the welfare of all nations'. His case was reported at length in March 1916:

Mr Crosland: Can you produce any evidence to show that this belief is not of recent date?

Applicant: Yes, I can produce sufficient evidence to convince this Tribunal. I could produce women and men to show that for many years I have advocated anti-militarist views and the sacredness of human life.

Mr Crosland: You are against militarism. I am against it too, and always have been. That is no reason why you should not go to fight or your country.

Applicant: I have no country.

Mr Crosland: What are you doing here, having no country? Why are you receiving all the benefits of a citizen when you have no country?

Applicant: Whatever benefits I am receiving have only been got by the organised workers wringing them from the master class. I am here this afternoon defending one of the liberties we at present enjoy, the liberty of conscience.

(Mr Crosland suggested non-combatant service)

The Mayor: He objects to combatant and to non-combatant, and he objects on conscientious grounds.

Applicant: My objection is not only to killing another man, but also to making ammunition.

The Mayor: You don't object to shelter here behind the brave men who are fighting?

Applicant: I am quite prepared to leave the country if you allow me to do so.

Mr Crosland: There are people who would be very glad to get rid of you if you would pay your own expenses.

Applicant: I am prepared to pay my own if you will allow me to leave the country.

The Mayor: You might be getting 'out of the frying pan and into the fire'. What country would you go to?

Applicant: I don't think I should tell the Tribunal. It is immaterial which country I would go to.

The Mayor: Go to Germany perhaps?

Applicant: Perhaps so. I might not be any worse off than I am here.

Mr Crosland: I think you are talking through your hat.

'I have no country'. Conscientious objector Arthur Gardiner.

Applicant: That is a matter of opinion.

Mr Crosland: This conscientious objection is an unsubstantial thing.

Applicant: No, conscience is a material thing. You might not be able to understand it, other people perhaps can…

(There was a pause) Applicant: I realise the interests of the workers of Germany are identical with those of the workers of England, and for that reason I cannot march against them and will not.

Mr Crosland: And you will not do non-combatant service?

Applicant: Certainly not.

The Mayor: They are fighting against England!

Applicant: No, they are not fighting against me.

The Mayor: Well, you are a unit in this empire.

Applicant: No; I don't think my name has been brought up at all in the German Reichstag. (Laughter)

The Mayor: It would have been absurd to do so.

Applicant: Certainly it would. It is not my fault that I was born here. I am neither to be praised nor blamed for it…

On the return of the Tribunal the mayor said they had had some difficulty in coming to a decision, but they had decided by a majority, and the decision was that they believed that the applicant was entitled to call himself a conscientious objector. They were very sorry that a man of his attainments and ability could not see the interests of his country at the present time were in an opposite direction, but in view of the fact that they believed the sincerity of his convictions, they were disposed to grant temporary exemption for two months.

'Report on the Huddersfield Tribunal',
The Worker, 25 March 1916

Such temporary exemptions on political grounds passed the decision to the higher level tribunals. Not all, however, convinced the panels of their sincerity. Those whose appeal failed were now legally in the Army, and subject to military law. Failure to report for duty meant being absent without leave and, in the Army, that was a criminal offence.

There were about thirty men in a room designed for fifteen. The stench of humanity and drunks was nothing to the crowning stench of a filthy latrine in the corner, of which the drain was choked and urine was seeping across the guardroom floor. I had to pick a dry patch. I did not feel happy, nor that I was suffering in a noble cause. I knew that these inconveniences were paltry compared with the sufferings brought to millions by the cursed war, but coming from an ideal home it was bad enough. Two blankets had been doled out, one for mattress and one for cover, but I had no pillow. I had brought my Teacher's Bible, which for many years had given light and strength. This served as a pillow.

Bert Brocklesby, Conisbrough, Remand Cell at Pontefract Barracks

From then on, it was a battle of wills between the absolutists and the military authorities. In one case raised in Parliament, a conscientious objector posted to a remount depot in England, responsible for preparing horses and mules for service overseas, refused to sweep out a horse's stall on the grounds that 'it had a distinct bearing on the prosecution of the war'. Others refused to peel potatoes in camp kitchens in England for the same reason.

I remember Father asking me what work I was prepared to do, if any. I said I would sew mailbags. He asked if that was not also war work as they would be used to carry letters for the soldiers. I said I saw no harm in soldiers having letters from home.

Bert Brocklesby

The military, however, could not allow soldiers to pick and choose what orders they were prepared to obey. For those who were posted to France, failure to obey a direct order was a serious offence and could result in 'Field Punishment Number One'. This involved the offender being attached to a fixed object such as a gun wheel or a fence post for up to two hours per day, three days out of four, for up to twenty-one days at a Field Punishment camp. While this was the standard military punishment for a wide variety of offences and was applied to all soldiers, supporters of conscientious objectors widely used the term 'crucifixion' as a way of making a punishment for a criminal offence into noble suffering for their cause. Alfred Evans, who would eventually be sentenced to death (later commuted) for his repeated refusal to obey orders, claimed that 'it was very uncomfortable, but certainly not humiliating'. It became almost a badge of honour.

For many, perhaps the majority, of men in the forces and for their families at home, the implied moral superiority of men who felt that the law should not apply to them made a mockery of the patriotism and loyalty of those who were serving. That loyalty was about to be tested to the limit on a previously quiet sector of the Western Front.

In June 1915, the French Commander-in-Chief, General Joffre, had proposed that the Allies (France, Great Britain, Belgium, Italy,

Serbia and Russia) should begin to co-ordinate their efforts in a more effective way, and so the First Inter-Allied Military Conference took place at Chantilly on 7 July 1915. By November, the Prime Ministers of France and Great Britain agreed to form a permanent committee to coordinate action. Soon after that, Joffre proposed simultaneous large-scale attacks with maximum forces by French, British, Italian and Russian troops as soon as conditions were favourable in the New Year. Until then, each army would continue to wear down the German and Austro-Hungarian forces by 'vigorous action'.

On 20 January 1916, Joffre told the newly appointed General Douglas Haig that by the end of April he would have five offensives prepared. Three would be in the south-east, one in the Champagne and one on the Oise-Somme front as discussed, but which one would be selected as the main thrust would depend on the military situation at the time. Meanwhile it would be important for the enemy to be pinned down and requested that Haig attack north of the Somme on a large scale – a minimum 7-mile front – around mid-April 1916. The plan had no strategic intent but was simply to cause as much damage as possible to the enemy as part of a war of attrition. Haig said he could not agree: his forces would not be ready, it would be politically unacceptable at home and it would be regarded by the British public as a failed attack. After further discussion, Joffre agreed to change the plan, deciding that a combined Franco-British offensive should be carried out across the Somme sometime that summer, with a smaller attack by the British in the area between La Bassee and Ypres. The French Sixth Army would place a corps north of the river, to act as a flank for his larger attack to the south of it. Haig, aware of the recent developments in the design of the tank, hoped to wait until August so that he could use them to maximum effect in the British attack.

Unfortunately, on 21 February 1916, the Germans struck a mighty blow against the French at Verdun and by the 26th it was clear that this was not a limited effort. The German commander, Falkenhayn, had set out to 'bleed France white' by attacking the symbolically crucial forts at Verdun, intending to draw the French army into a battle whose sole purpose would be to kill as many Frenchmen as possible. On 3 March, Joffre asked Haig to do all he could to divert German reserves away from the battle, if necessary by launching the Somme offensive early. By the end of the month, Haig's senior, General William 'Wullie' Robertson, pressed the British Government for instructions about what they wanted Haig to do. On 7 April, approval was given for British involvement in the Somme offensive.

On 29 May, at the suggestion of Haig, Robertson reminded the government that in view of the small number of French and British Divisions available for the offensive, far-reaching results should not be expected. The idea of a simultaneous Allied attack with maximum force was no longer a possibility and the most that could be achieved would be to inflict enough damage on the Germans that they would have to pull back from their attacks at Verdun. Two days later, having been informed that Verdun was about to fall, Haig told his French colleagues that the British would be ready to play their part. On 3 June, he received orders from Joffre that he must attack at the end of the month.

Many of Haig's men were the untried Kitchener volunteers of the Pals Battalions. He was concerned that their training had been improvised, and that very few of their officers had any real battle experience. This was a particular problem given the limited means of communication available to senior commanders. Radios were not yet advanced enough to be portable and the only way to get messages to and from a unit in the attack was by carrier pigeon or by a written message carried by runners. Both took time and meant that it was vitally important to keep men together, so that platoons did not lose contact with each other.

The failure of the British offensive at Loos in 1915 had taught valuable lessons that had been incorporated into a manual published on 8 May 1916, which described using successive waves of troops to drive home the attack, reach the objective and have the ability to prepare captured ground against counter attack (defences, for example, would need to be reversed and the layout of trenches turned around). To achieve this, and to avoid exhausting troops, eight waves, each about 100 yards apart, would attack so that the lead wave would only need to fight for a few minutes before fresh troops arrived to take over. Platoons would be divided up into different functions – some would do the fighting, some would 'mop-up' (clear the trenches of any remaining defenders after the main fighting). Others would be 'support' and 'carrying' units, bringing the tools, ammunition and heavy weapons needed to establish control of the newly captured trenches. Troops in carrying platoons might have to carry thirty kilograms of kit, soldiers in the first waves would carry a rifle, bayonet, 170 rounds of ammunition, iron rations of bully beef and biscuits, two hand grenades, a pick, shovel or entrenching tool, four empty sandbags, gas helmet, wire cutters and a water bottle. Although considerably lighter than the support platoon's load, this was still a burden and orders were issued to advance at a steady pace so that men did not arrive at their objective too tired to fight. The order, though, was not set in stone. Brigade and even battalion commanders were able to make their own decisions about how their men would advance, based on what they felt best suited the area they were operating in.

On 16 June, Haig explained his intentions for the coming offensive: to relieve pressure on the French at Verdun and to inflict losses on the German army. Aware that these were the limits of the French demands, Haig had formulated a plan, that with luck could lead to a breakthrough, but knew the chances were slim. General Rawlinson, who commanded the Fourth Army, was wary of asking too much of untried troops and took a more cautious view, looking only for small advances onto high ground and pauses to consolidate, ready for German counter-attacks.

We must remember that owing to a large expansion of our army and the heavy casualties in experienced officers, the officers and troops generally do not now possess that military knowledge arising from a long and high state of training which enables them to react instinctively and promptly on sound lines in unexpected situations. They have become accustomed to deliberate action based on detailed orders … They [should] push forward at a steady pace in successive lines, each line adding impetus to the preceding line. Although a steady pace for assaulting troops is recommended, occasions may arise where the rapid advance of some lightly equipped men on some particular part of the enemy's defences may turn the scale.

Fourth Army Instructions, 1916

After three months in Egypt, the Bradford, Leeds, Barnsley, Sheffield and Hull Pals of 31st Division set sail for Marseilles in early March 1916 in high spirits. Not everyone, though, was eager to reach France.

We had a Major Norman, who had been in France, been slightly wounded and then they sent him out to join us, and he says to me, he says, 'you know Dalby, I'm not going back there, I don't give a so-and-so if I get cashiered, he said I'm not going back to France, I've had enough'. Course he was a regular, he had trench warfare and he'd had as much as he wanted.

He got cashiered, he got drunk and fell into Sweetwater Canal that runs alongside the Suez Canal. He told me himself, 'I'm not going back, if I get cashiered I'm not going back'. I don't know what happened to him, he disappeared, that's all I know about him.

Private Arthur Dalby, Leeds Pals

After a quiet trip, the Division arrived in France in March 1916 to find the cold and wet of France a terrible shock after their time in the sun.

Troops moving forward to the Somme. For the Yorkshire Pals, fresh from Egypt, the march was to prove tortuous.

Men were falling out right and left with blistered and sore feet. Evidently Egypt had not done us much good, for every man was exhausted when we reached Longpre…

Private J. W. Graystone, Hull Commercials

Saturday 25 March – Reveille 5 a.m. Everything cleared away and billets cleaned up. Parade at 9 a.m. – pack very heavy. Arrived Arraines 12.30 p.m. 8 miles … Feet very sore with new boots. Sunday 26 March – … Feet terribly sore and having a very bad time – murder marching…. Monday 27 March – Reveille 5 a.m. … Feet very bad to start off and became gradually worse. Absolute torture. Passed through Flesselles, Talmas. Feet horribly bad – after great effort compelled to fall out…

'Diary of Private John Yeadon', Leeds Pals

As they prepared to go into the trenches for the first time, a new bit of kit was handed out. In response to the number of head injuries among troops in the trenches, John Leopold Brodie had designed a bowl-shaped helmet that could deflect shrapnel and shell splinters.

The original design had been improved by the use of Hadfield Steel, made in Sheffield, after staff at Hadfields borrowed a pattern for soup bowls in order to develop a helmet that gave greater protection than the ordinary steel first used.

I think it was at Bus [Bus-les-Artois] that we were first issued with tin hats. It was strange at first trying to balance a steel bowl on your head, but like other Army ways we got used to them and felt that nothing could harm us now. One night, soon after we got them, I went out in front as a covering party for a wiring job. As I lay outstretched, I took my tin hat off and propped it up, stuck it in the earth in front of me, got behind it and felt as safe as houses.

Private Arthur Pearson, Leeds Pals

The first experiences of trench warfare for the newly arrived Pals was in marked contrast to that of the Territorials the previous year:

It was my first time in the trenches, and Matthews took me in hand and gave me cheery advice, promising to keep an eye on me and answer my questions. Later when the bombardment commenced, he got me at his side. The parapet was blown in and buried me completely, but I found I was still getting air through a small hole and so called for help. Matthews was surprised to find I was alive I think, and set about to try and extricate me. He found the weight too great, so discovered my air hole and scraped at it for some time. This gave me more scope for breathing. To this act I think I owe my life. The hole supplied me with air for about an hour and a half, when a working party found me on hearing my call. While your son was clearing out the hole his hand found mine and with a strong grip on it he assured me that he would get me out somehow. At this moment I heard a loud bang and the hand went limp in mine. I cannot express how sorry I am at being the cause of this sad accident but believe me I shall always think with gratitude of my one time comrade and his noble sacrifice on my behalf.

Private Leonard McIvor, 12th York and Lancasters, writing to the parents of Robert Matthews following an incident on 16 May 1916. McIvor was killed on 1 July 1916, aged twenty-four

For the next few weeks, the various Pals units took turns in the trenches until early June when they were withdrawn to begin training for their role in the coming offensive. Forming the left flank of the British offensive, 31st Division was to attack on a 1,000-yard front with 94th Brigade (Sheffield, Barnsley and Accrington Pals) on the left and 93rd

Brigade (Durham, Bradford and Leeds Pals) on the right. Behind them, 92nd Brigade (Hull Pals) would remain in reserve until called forward. Training began in earnest on 14 June, when clocks were put forward an hour to allow extra daylight.

A five-day bombardment was planned to break down the German morale and to try to cut the swathes of barbed wire in no man's land to make paths for the troops to walk through. Over 1.5 million shells rained down on the enemy trenches in what they came to call *trommelfeuer,* since the rapid explosions seemed to blend into a sound like a drum roll.

It started then. It started with the little 'uns and then the big 'uns, and then 'crash', on for days. I think it lasted about seven days, you couldn't tell to the exact day because it was at it night and day and God love me, you didn't know where to put yourself. You were absolutely muddled with the bloody things. Bang, bang, bang, bang. Behind us there were some Navy guns on wagons on a railway line.

Private Frank Lindley, 14th York and Lancaster

When orders came through for the advance, we had a miniature of the German trenches and points which we were to take in our particular sector. The company officers assembled the NCOs and explained to them from maps the whole position and our objective, and the NCOs passed this information on to every man, so that no casualties should interrupt the progress of the battalion. We had to reach the fourth line of the German trenches and there consolidate, which meant reversing the trench so that the high side becomes the low side.

Corporal James Thompson, Leeds Pals

We knew a bit about it before, because they took us out into the country behind the lines and they had it all threaded out … They had red lines, blue lines, tapes and they drew a map by tapes and pegs of our objective. Now, when you get to that red line, wait until the next one. When you get to that blue line wait. This was alright in theory by the headquarters, but when you come to do anything in practice, theory goes out the window.

Private Clifford Hollingworth, Leeds Pals

Across the Somme front, similar exercises were being held. Serving with 21st Division, the troops of the KOYLI were warned,

The use of the word 'retire' is absolutely forbidden in this Division. All ranks are distinctly to understand that if such an order is given, it is either a device of the enemy, or it is given by some person who has lost his head. In any case this order is never to be obeyed.

'Order No 36', issued to 9th Battalion KOYLI, June 1916

As the day of the attack approached, the thunder of the British artillery barrage convinced many that few of the German defenders would be left alive but men prepared for the worst:

My very, very dearest Mother, I feel I ought to write you all something in the nature of a farewell in case I should not return to you from this war. You'll understand the difficulty I have in writing a letter you will not read till I am no more, and that there is so much that I would like to say, it is exceedingly hard to say it. I will begin by trying to explain what have been my feelings ever since I came out here but more pronounced now than ever before. I believe I do not fear death – at least I hope not and tell myself I do not; but I am a coward for I do fear pain. I will not dwell on the idea of receiving some horrible wound; but worse than all, I fear causing you to suffer pain – pain which I know would be mental rather than physical, and for that reason the greater. So if there is an afterlife in which we can still take notice of and interest in the things that happen in this world, nothing would cause me greater trouble than to see you, after my death, stricken down by grief. Of course I know the measure of your sorrow would be the measure of your love for me – and so I do not ask that you should not grieve for me, only that you should not be overcome and dominated by your grief. All I can do myself is assure you that I have gone into this great adventure loving you with all my heart and with all my soul, further that the great love which I have for you has kept me straight – has almost been my God. I cannot tell you what my feelings are on religion – I do not yet know myself – all I can say is that I am not a Christian in the true sense of the word, but I am not an atheist. I believe in some good God – more I cannot say, or, at any rate, write. I know nothing – what mortal really knows anything – of a future life; but I trust that we shall in some state hereafter all meet again ... I will not speak of patriotism and sacrifice except to say this: I am sure that had I hung back when our country said it needed all its youth, I should have disappointed you, though I realise that your sacrifice is greater than mine: I am only offering my life, you have offered your love: and while I have been so busied, and even pleasantly busied and so have little time for cares, it has been your lot – the harder one – to sit at home and suffer anxiety in silence ... If I die in this war, I did so knowing that I can do no better thing – and what finer consummation of all that I have been brought up to think good and noble can I wish for?

Lieutenant G. F. Ellenberger, 9th Battalion KOYLI, 25 June 1916

My own Darling Mother and Father, In the event of my getting a clean knockout blow from the Hun, Monier [his elder brother] will send you this letter. I just wanted to tell you that I do not fear death except insofar as everyone must fear it, viz, undergoing some experience which one has never had before. But I just want you both to remember this one thing, after all, what is death? Death to my mind is simply a gateway through which one passes into Life, I mean real Life. We merely exist in this world, in the world to come we shall LIVE. We are all bound to come to this gateway called death sooner or later. Whether it is sooner or later can really matter very little to any of us. Simply because in thirty of forty years the whole family will be together for ever in eternal life. And what is thirty or forty years together in this world compared to the endless ages we shall all spend together in the life to come. If you look at it in this light, death has no terror, and really very little sorrow or grief attached to it. At least you should feel none of these things. Both of you will have to die sooner or later. If Mother dies first, you Dad will know that I shall be waiting at the gate to give her a welcome. And if Dad dies then you, Mother darling, will know that Dad and I are waiting for you; isn't that just splendid? At any rate this is what I believe, and I believe it because you two, by your dear lives, have taught us all to believe in Jesus Christ the Son of God, who died that we might live. Don't forget that I shall be loving you both at the moment you are reading this, just as dearly as I do now while writing it. Ever your own Loving son.

Lt S. Morris, Bickersteth, Leeds Pals

My dearest Dad and Mother. The advance has come at last and early tomorrow we shall attack. I am in command of the front line of my Company and it is the very first line of attack. If I come through I shall be able to tell you about our part of the greatest battle that ever will be. If I should be killed you must not fret, as it is the finest death to die, and I have no fear in meeting it. I must stop now. With love, Ralph.

2nd Lieutenant Ralph Stead, Bradford Pals

Just a line to say I go 'over the lid' tomorrow. My company are in the first line of attack and hope to do great things. We all naturally hope to come through all right, but of course, one never knows, someone's bound to go under and it's the only way to end the war. It's a great thing to be in, and I'm glad our division is one of the first chosen to go over.

Lieutenant Robert Sutcliffe, Bradford Pals

[Lt General Hunter Weston] stood on a box and made a speech to us. He went on about having the true 'attack' spirit and the old words about fighting

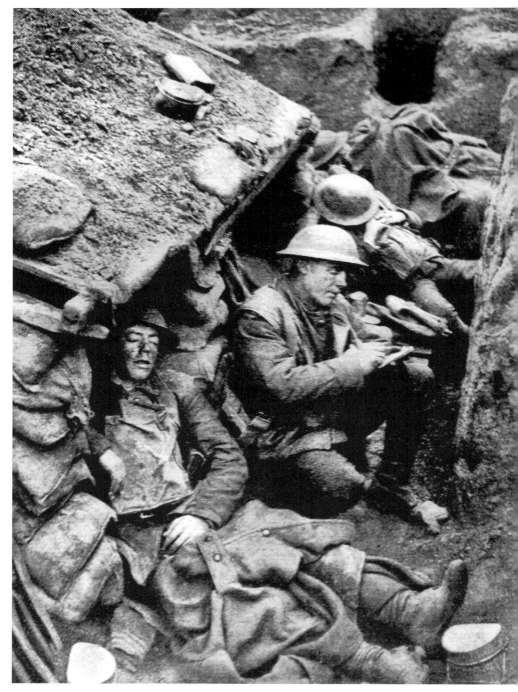

Troops moving forward to the Somme. For the Yorkshire Pals, fresh from Egypt, the march was to prove tortuous.

for Britain's honour came out. He said the Germans were barbarians who didn't understand honour and it was the Germans who had started the war. We were to have no doubts in our minds about which side was fighting for a just cause. God was on our side and the only good German was a dead one … all that sort of stuff. He went on like that for some time. He told us not to worry because not even a rat would be left alive in the German trenches after our bombardment. Then he said something which made us all very angry. He said anyone who funked the attack and didn't go forward would be shot on the spot. He said there were plenty of military police about in the trenches and they had strict orders to watch for any shirkers. We felt sickened by this sort of talk. What sort of men did he think we were? ... he then rode off to raise the morale of some other battalion. They led us to believe it was just going to be tea-party. Some bloody tea-party.

Private George Morgan, Bradford Pals

I remember some bigwig came and spoke to us, all decked out in medals. He gave us some sort of pep talk and that we were for it. After it was over the band played 'When You Come to the End of a Perfect Day'. What a bloody tune to play.

Private D. C. Cameron, Sheffield City Battalion

I had always been a churchgoer. In fact I sang in the Sheffield Cathedral choir, boy and man, so I thought I would go for communion before the battle. Up to that point the forthcoming event hadn't bothered me, but at that church service held in the wood, seeing as we could the build up of marching men, guns and horses moving towards the front, then I had this feeling of awe. It must have been the effects of the service and seeing all this movement that you got this feeling, just as if something was coming at you.

Corporal Douglas Edward Cattell, Sheffield City Battalion

Our last evening in the village [Bus-les-Artois] was like a gala night at Roundhay Park. There was the band on the green; there was the hearty laughter and the insistent burr of the broad West Riding twang; and there was much talk of Briggate and Boar Lane and the Saturday morning Bond Street 'crawl'. But we missed the Yorkshire lasses - and there were no French desmoiselles available as partners for the dance. Yet it was a rollicking night – a night that those of us who survive will remember as long as memory lives.

Private Lance Grocock, Leeds Pals

Although I cannot remember all the programme played on that lovely summer evening so long ago, I certainly have an abiding memory of one piece, Schubert's Unfinished Symphony. Because of this, every performance that I have heard of it

129

Church service before battle.

since takes me back to that evening in Bus, still quite clear, in my mind's eye, with all those Leeds and Bradford Pals sitting around on the grass quietly listening, and with all of them no doubt wondering, as I certainly did, what waited us at daybreak the following morning.

Private William Slater, Bradford Pals

At about 6 p.m. on 28 June all officers received a summons to go to Battalion HQ for a final drink before going into action. We assembled, glasses were put into our hands, drinks were passed round and we drank quietly to one another – everyone was naturally feeling strained. The Adjutant and Second-in-command were away on some course, so the Acting Adjutant, Keay, was in charge. Lynch came into the room and was given a glass. Keay went up to Haswell, the senior Captain, and said quietly to him, 'I think you should propose the CO's health!' 'I'm damned if I will', said Haswell 'I don't wish him good health and am not prepared to be insincere on this occasion'. 'You must', said Keay. 'I won't' , said Haswell. For a few moments they argued, and then Haswell stepped forward and raising his glass said: 'Gentlemen, I give you the toast of the King's Own Yorkshire Light Infantry, and in particular the 9th Battalion of the Regiment' – a slight pause – 'Gentleman, when the barrage lifts…' We emptied our glasses and were silent. Dramatically, Haswell had avoided an unpleasant scene, and the toast has never been forgotten.

Lieutenant Lancelot Spicer, 9th KOYLI

Two nights before, oh yes, we'd had a free for all in the market square with a band and one of the privates took the baton from the bandmaster and oh, we'd had a real time. The French people brought their beer out, we'd brought ours. We got them sozzled on our beer and we were up all night with their beer, but I don't know if it was a good thing because it was supposed to be hush-hush was this. The Germans knew what was going on. As a matter of fact when I was taken prisoner of war, I met a man who was on that front and he said they'd been expecting it for a week.

Private Clifford Hollingworth, Leeds Pals

In fact, the Germans were fully expecting the attack. The build-up of forces was hard to disguise and the wet soil of the Somme acted as a conductor, allowing the Germans to listen in to telephone messages along the British lines whose calls had been intercepted for some time. The only piece missing from the jigsaw was the time.

Battalion set off in good spirits. Wish I was going with them.

Private Fred Rawnsley Bradford Pals,
'Diary Entry' 30 June 1916

He was a nice lad, was Henderson, and from what I can gather, you know them water buckets that horses have? They had grenades and bombs in them and he was taking one out … as he put it in [his pocket] it triggered off … course once you trigger one off the whole lot goes. So of course he was killed and all the chaps around him were thrown on their backs … So we lost thirty-five men that night before we went up.

Private Clifford Hollingsworth, Leeds Pals

At 6 p.m. on the last day of June, the long march into the assembly trenches began.

The feeling of comradeship among us seemed to grow as we marched forward into a common danger. In particular I have a lasting memory of the man who was closest to me as we marched. I was only eighteen at the time, having joined the army under age, and he was some years older than I. As he spoke to me,

I became aware of a feeling of tenderness in him towards me, as though he sensed my fears and was trying to reassure both himself and me. 'Don't worry Bill', he said, 'we'll be all right'. And he spoke as gently as a mother trying to soothe a frightened child.

Private William Slater, Bradford Pals

Opposite the fortified village of Serre, 31st Division's assembly trenches followed the edge of four small copses, nicknamed Matthew, Mark, Luke and John. At about 4 a.m. German artillery fire suddenly intensified.

We went down the line about 4 o'clock and got our places in the front trench, with C Company in the front trench and following up was A Company … the ground was just like an upheaval, you could hear nothing for the noise of the shelling.

Private Morrison Fleming, Leeds Pals

I was afraid – everyone must have been afraid, but I was more afraid of showing it. I didn't want to let the side down. I hoped I would be able to do what I was expected to do.

Private George Morgan, Bradford Pals

My feelings were very mixed as we waited to go over. More so with us because we'd had no experience at all from a fighting point of view. We were wondering what it would be like. We had no idea that it would be like it turned out to be.

Private Tommy Oughton, Barnsley Pals

We knew what time they were going to blow the whistles, half past seven. We knew it all before we started, it was passed down somehow. I can remember thinking what was going to happen when we went over. The birds were singing and the sun came up. It was a beautiful day, beautiful. We had the morning chorus before we had the 'other'.

Private Frank Lindley, Barnsley Pals.

You could hear the larks at five minutes to seven. You could hear nothing else after that.

Private Vernon Atkinson, Barnsley Pals

There was no lingering about when zero hour came. Our platoon officer [twenty-year-old 2nd Lieutenant Frank Symonds] blew the whistle and he was the first up the scaling ladder with his revolver in one hand and a cigarette in the other. 'Come on, boys', he said and up he went. We went up after him one at a time. I never saw the officer again. He was reported missing and his name is on the Thiepval Memorial. He was only young but he was a very very brave man. Private George Morgan, Bradford Pals. When the whistle went we went up the ladders and began walking across towards Serre, but we were still among our own trenches ... As I jumped across one trench I saw my first casualty that morning, it was the top half of a man – the other half was lying in the bottom of the trench. I don't know if he were a Barnsley lad or a Sheffielder, he must have taken the full blast of the shell. Sheffield City Battalion had been in the front line of trenches. They must have been wiped out by this time.

Private Charlie Swales, Barnsley Pals

If the English thought they could wear us out by the unprecedented fire of the past few days they were badly mistaken ... Now everyone knows that the hour of retaliation will soon come. Cartridges and hand grenade reserves are made ready...the alarm call 'They are coming!' is screamed in the dugouts ... Over there in closed rifle ranks, came the attacking English. Slowly, almost leisurely, they trot along, out of the third into the second, then into the first English trench. From there they proceed into the attack, their light cooking utensils flash in the gunpowder impregnated air.

History of the 169th German Infantry Regiment, Serre

For some reason nothing seemed to happen to us. At first we strolled along as though walking in a park. Then suddenly, we were in the midst of a storm of machine gun bullets and I saw men beginning to twirl round and fall in all kinds of curious ways as they were hit, quite unlike the way actors do it in films.

Private William Slater, Bradford Pals

When the English started advancing we were very worried; they looked as though they must overrun our trenches. We were very surprised to see them walking, we had never seen that before. I could see them everywhere; there were hundreds... When we started firing, we just had to load and reload. They went down in their hundreds. You didn't have to aim, we just fired into them. If only they had run, they would have overwhelmed us ... here was a wailing and lamentation from No Man's Land and much shouting for stretcher bearers from the stricken English. They lay in piles but those who survived fired at us from behind their bodies. Later on, when the English tried again, they weren't walking this time, they were running as fast as they could but when they reached the pile of bodies they got no farther. I could see English officers gesticulating wildly, trying to call their reserves forward, but very few came. Normally after 5000 rounds had been fired we changed the barrel of the machine gun. We changed it five times that morning.

Musketier Karl Blenk, 169th Regiment, at Serre

Troops go over the lid.

The whistle blew and over we went. One or two of our lads had dropped down, they were dropping all around us, and one that had dropped was screaming out, his leg was in a bad way. I knelt down to pull his puttees off and his boot, he'd been badly smashed in the leg, and up behind me then come Major Booth … and he said to me 'What are you doing? Come on, it doesn't matter about him, it's onward you go, come on, get hold', and he got hold of me, lifted me up and the pair of us went forward. The Jerry was up with his machine-guns firing at us from a distance of about fifteen yards ahead of us. There were two shell holes open, one was on the right, in the wire, and one was on the left. He said, 'Come on, make for it'. I made for one shell hole and he made for further on. He'd got about a few yards and there was a shell burst and it was just one mass of bodies and one thing and another flying up in the air. I dropped myself in a shell hole … the memory's terrible … I got in the shell hole and that's where I stuck. I'd a spot on my arm it was just cut and a bullet through … the top of my leg. I was unconscious laid in that trench and that's where I laid the whole day. I could see the bodies going up in the air. A terrible sight, a sight that I'll never forget and the ground was like an upheaval, one mass of flame everywhere.

Anyway the night come along and I managed to get alongside one of our lads, he seemed to be alright, we managed to get back into the line. There was very few of us left, I think about four of us…

Private Morrison Fleming, Leeds Pals

I hadn't gone far before I was hit, being shot in the chest. I immediately rolled into a shell hole for better protection and imagine I lost consciousness for some considerable time. When I came to, I heard a voice and discovered there was another fellow in a shell hole about fifteen yards away, so I decided to join him. It was while crawling across that I got shot through the arm by a sniper. How long we were in that shell hole I don't know, for it must have been several days – we were parched with thirst and welcomed the heavy rain that came and which we collected in our steel helmets … All at once the other fellow decided to crawl in and off he went. That was the last I saw or heard of him. I decided then that it was impossible to stay out day after day and started to crawl in myself. I found it an agonizing and exhausting job, and have no idea how long it took me. Eventually I got into an old disused trench. Here I discovered a dugout and turned in. All I wanted was rest and oblivion, and I slept … In the dugout I found some bits of Army biscuits, and these soaked in rain water were the only food I had. I was absolutely too weak to do anything but lie and sleep, and did not move except when I crawled to get water. To sum matters up I was hit on 1 July and was discovered on the 15th.

Private Arthur Cecil Stagg, Sheffield Pals

Lieutenant Stead was in C Company. I saw him in the charge at Colincamps at 8.00am on July 1, 1916. He was wounded in the knee and was told to go back. He refused to go down and got up to lead the lads again but was shot down by [machine gun] fire. He was very young and very brave.

Private Harry Laycock, Bradford Pals.

Five minutes before 7.25am, the enemy Machine Gun, Rifle Fire and Shrapnel were directed against the parapet of our Assembly trench – the Southern half of Bradford Trench – causing us to suffer considerably. A lot of men never got off the ladder, but fell back; and many men fell back from the parapet, in getting over. On getting out of the trenches to take up our position in front we lost heavily through the line of shrapnel, machinegun and rapid rifle fire; by the time we attained our position in front of Bradford Trench, most of the officers, NCOs and many men were knocked out.

At Zero we advanced and continued to advance until the Company Headquarters with which I was found ourselves in front of the Battalion – all in front having been hit. We found ourselves then halfway between 'Leeds' and the front line. At this point I continued the advance – Capt. Smith having been knocked out – and I carried on until we reached the front line. In our advance we passed the majority of 'A' Co. Halfway between Leeds trench and the front line, lying on the ground, killed or wounded. I found in the front line a good many of the 15th W.Yorks, what was left of the [Durham Light Infantry] Co. Attached to us, also a few of the King's Own Yorkshire Light Infantry I found no officers or NCOs of any of the above regiments or of my own regiment.

After Action Report, Sergeant Major Cussins, 16th West Yorkshires

Sir, my duty as Intelligence Officer is not yet finished; I must try to let you know what went on up to the time of my being hit. At five minutes to zero, Major Guyon, Ransome and myself left our headquarters for the front line, followed closely by our retinue. We had only been by Sap A about two minutes when Major Guyon was struck through the helmet by a bullet. Ransome and I were alongside at the time and bandaged him up, though unconscious and apparently dying, the wound being in the temple. We were obliged to leave as things did not appear to be going well. We urged the men on and saw columns advancing over 'Leeds' Trench, one being led by Capt Pringle.

Things seemed to stop, men were falling and no-one advancing over our front line. Stead was in the front line with a few men, which we scraped together for a rush. Stead and I scrambled out and the men tried to follow but were mown down by machine gun fire. I got about fifteen yards before being hit by a bullet in the left knee and a piece of shrapnel in the right thigh, and managed to crawl to a shell hole about five yards in front where I found Stead, shot dead. After staying there for about fifteen minutes I tried to regain our trenches leaving all surplus kit and gained a shell hole a few yards nearer. Ransome evidently saw me and came out to my assistance.

I sent him back to find the nearest place where I could crawl into the trench, which he did, and I followed. This was the last I saw of him, but afterwards heard he was suffering from shell shock, with Hoffman. About any other Officer or Men I know nothing. I don't think our rear two Companies ever reached our frontline owing to the sweeping machine gun fire. I think these are all the details I can supply and hope things are going alright ... Hoping all is well. Your obedient servant

2nd Lt C. F. Claxton, 16th West Yorkshires,
'Report written from Hospital' 3 July 1916

7.40 a.m. – Barrage lifted from the German front line and first and second waves moved forward into the assault. They were immediately met with very heavy machine gun and rifle fire and artillery barrage. The left half of 'C' Company was wiped out before getting near the German wire and on the right the few men who reached the wire were unable to get through ... A great many casualties were caused by the enemy's machine guns; in fact the third and fourth waves suffered so heavily that by the time they reached No Man's Land they had lost at least half their strength. Whole sections were wiped out...

War Diary, 12th York and Lancaster, Sheffield Pals

7.00 a.m. – Although this advance had to be carried out under a perfect tornado of fire all ranks advanced as steadily as if on a drill parade ...

9 a.m. – While these two Companies were moving forward they were stopped by orders from the Brigadier who had now received information that all our preceding waves had been decimated and had consequently not reached their objectives ...

5 p.m. – 'C' Company was sent to relieve the survivors of 'A' Company who had been holding our front line and they were withdrawn to MONK TRENCH. The available strength of the Battalion at this time was about 280 all ranks.

'War Diary', 13th York and Lancaster Regiment, 1st Barnsley Pals

On the left flank, particularly between Nairne and John Copse it is estimated that 30 per cent of the assaulting, consolidating and clearing parties became casualties before reaching our parapet ... [of the 70 per cent who were able to leave the British trench] it would appear that barely 20 per cent were able to reach the German front line...

'War Diary', 14th York and Lancaster Regiment, 2nd Barnsley Pals

Wild firing slammed into the masses of the enemy. All around us was the rushing, whistling and roaring of a storm. Throughout all this racket could be heard the regular tack tack of the machine guns. Belt after belt was fired ... "Pass up the spare barrels" shouts the gun commander ... The barrel must be changed again, it is red hot and the cooling water is boiling ... The enemy closes up nearer, we fire on endlessly, the British keep charging forward..' Despite the fact that hundreds are already lying dead, fresh waves keep emerging from the assault trenches ... The British have closed to grenade throwing range and grenades fly backwards and forwards...

Unteroffizer Otto Lais, 169th Regiment

For the survivors and the wounded, there was little to do but take cover. Those who could crawled back to the British lines, many more would have to wait for darkness before they could make the terrible journey.

It was a drag, dragging at the side of the trenches. It really didn't seem too far. I was sliding over different people that had been done in the other trenches. They'd caught it as bad as we had at the front. While we'd been getting dealt with up there, the Germans had been dealing with the other lot behind us. The reserve lines were peppered. There were no reserves left, they were in a pulp. One bloke must have been climbing out of the trench and it had done him across the middle. It left his feet and bottom half in the trench and all his insides were hanging down the side of the trench. I remember thinking 'So that's what a liver and kidney look like'. It's funny what you think at times like that ... I got by and I got to the end of Nairne Street, and there was a bloke patching you up. It was a bit of an aid post. He had a go at me and gave me a shot for tetanus and then they picked us up and slotted us in a little ambulance feet first, on little shelves, and away we went. What I thought, mainly, the very first thing I thought was 'How the bloody hell are they going to clear this mess up?' Them stretcher bearers must have thought all Hell was let loose. With a disaster on the scale as it was you wondered how the hell they shifted 'em. There's a lot still there, there must be.

Private Frank Lindley, 14th York and Lancaster Regiment

From my shell hole I could see a dead man propped up against the German wire in a sitting position. He was sniped at during the day until his head was completely shot away.

Lieutenant Robert Heptonstall,
13th York and Lancaster Regiment

As far as I can make out, General, I have two companies left. If you would like me to charge at their head I shall be delighted to do so.

Colonel Wilford, Barnsley Pals, to Brigadier General Rees

I helped a stretcher bearer bind up Lieutenant Derwent's wound [2nd Lieutenant Rob Derwent, cub reporter and son of the Bradford Telegraph's Managing Director] which was just above the groin, shrapnel had gone right through and it bled a great deal. He had been wounded some hours and did not speak. He frothed at the mouth, folded his hands, stretched out his legs and fell away. Private Frank Smith, Bradford Pals. I managed to crawl half a mile to Basin Wood where I saw the most horrible sight. Our M[edical] O[fficer] [Capt Roche] was working at a trestle table in his vest, and bodies were piled like sandbags all around him.

Corporal Albert Wood, Bradford Pals

As the assault against Serre by the Pals of 31st Division faltered, other Yorkshire units were going into action across the 27,000-yard (15-mile) British front. Another 'New Army' Division, the 21st, included the 9th and 10th KOYLI, the 10th West Yorkshires, the 10th York and Lancasters and the 1st and 8th East Yorkshires. Their task was to attack around the fortified village of Fricourt, attempting to encircle it to cut off the defenders before capturing the village itself.

Next morning, Keay and I rose at 6.15 a.m. The attack was to start at 7.00 a.m. and the bombardment was already very intense. All we could hear was a steady dull roar, with an occasional loud boom, as some big shell was exported by our guns, or heavier crash as some large 'crump' was imported. Keay and I rode up to the hill between Ville and Morlancourt where we got off and left our horses with a groom. We walked over the fields till we got to a spot where we could see well over the German lines, and particularly the Poodles, Crucifix Trench, and Shelter Wood. To our dismay a thick mist hung over the lines, and we could see nothing. It was now about 7.20 a.m. and the bombardment was more intense than ever. We were both suffering badly from 'needle' and could barely keep still. The next ten minutes seemed eternity. At 7.20 a.m. we thought of the first wave crawling out and getting ready. Each minute a fresh wave would get out. At last 7.30 came. Almost simultaneously we could distinguish the patter-patter of the machine guns, and rifle fire. It did not seem very intense fire, but the sound was unmistakable. It did not last long, and we hoped for the best, but somehow or other the sound had seemed very ominous. We waited till 8.15 a.m. and then as the firing was becoming less intense, and we could see nothing, we went back.

The observation balloons had moved forward – some of them nearly half a mile. This seemed a good sign. During the morning we learnt nothing till about 11 a.m. when the wounded started returning. From then onwards we had the usual collection of rumours. The advance appeared to be going on, but it was impossible to find out definitely how far we had got. There seemed to be no doubt that the two King's Own Yorkshire Light Infantry battalions, tho' they had done magnificently, had had heavy losses. The C. O. was reported killed and so was Walker. Morris was wounded in the mouth – that seemed definite.

Lieutenant Lancelot Spicer, 9th KOYLI

The advance was by crawling and by rushes from shell hole to shell hole. The noise was deafening and the German machine gun fire was terrible. Just before reaching the Russian Sap I was struck on the chin by a bit of shrapnel. When I reached the sap I lay down and looked into it. I saw Colonel Lynch, who said: 'Hullo Gordon, are you hit?' I put my hand to my chin and found it was covered with blood. The Colonel began to get out of the sap. He was killed by a shell almost immediately afterwards ... By this time our waves were jumbled together and, owing to the smoke, it was difficult to keep direction ... after a few more minutes, which seemed ages, I reached the German front trenches. Several 'B' Company men joined me, and I sat in a shell hole while one of them bandaged my chin, which was cut and bruised and bleeding freely ... Although our bombardment had failed to knock out the enemy machine guns, its effect on their trenches had been great. For the most part they were entirely knocked in, one long succession of shell-holes, brown craters mainly, for the soil is thick. Now and then one came to an enormous white crater caused, I believe, by our trench mortars. These were fifteen or twenty feet deep and as many yards across.

Lieutenant B. L. Gordon, 9th KOYLI

The whole thing was so very fast and it was such hot work that you hadn't time to sit and think over the horrors, but just went on and on, pursued by a decided but unexpressed feeling that you would sooner be anywhere than here. The Hun ran, and we took a lot of prisoners; he has a very unsporting idea about fighting, has the Hun. He'll poop away with his machine gun at you, and he'll snipe at you, and he'll throw bombs at you, but as soon as you get to close quarters, with the bayonet, he puts up his hands ... I saw a lot of Huns, and a lot of Hun rifles, and it's an absolute fact that none of them had a fixed bayonet – when it comes to bayonet work they put up their hands; the bayonets we found afterwards down in the dugouts.

Lieutenant George Ellenberger, 9th KOYLI

Nearby was twenty-one-year-old Lieutenant Philip Howe of Sheffield, who had graduated from Sheffield University in the summer of 1914 and was invited in August to join the University Officer Training Corps. After just one month, he and several others decided instead to enlist as privates in the new Sheffield City Battalion. When it became obvious that the battalion would not be going into action soon, Howe applied for a commission. His law degree stood him in good stead as the desperate need for officers in the Kitchener Army battalions meant he was granted an immediate promotion and, without any training, found himself a Second Lieutenant in the 10th West Yorkshires. Ever eager, he would lead the attack on Fricourt.

The trenches we had to get out of were deep, and it was necessary to climb up ladders. Naturally this made us a bit slow, so the people who came up behind suffered many more casualties than those who got over first. I put down my survival to the fact that I was first over the top, and got almost as far as the German trenches before anything happened. I met a German officer whose idea was to attack us as we crossed no man's land and he was armed with a whole array of stick bombs which he proceeded to throw at me and I replied by trying to shoot my revolver. I missed every time and he missed with his stick bombs as well. After this had gone on for a few seconds – it seemed like hours – somebody kindly shot this German officer and I made my way to the place I was told to go originally, which was a map reference about a hundred yards behind the German front line.

I made my way to this little trench which I had seen by aerial photographs. I had started off with more or less the whole battalion, but I found myself in this trench with about twenty men. I had been shot through the hand and we quickly discovered that we were surrounded on all four sides. So I got all the men down in a dugout which had very steep sides and twenty steps leading down from the trench at the top to the dugout below. Just then another officer came along who had been shot through the leg and wasn't particularly mobile.

I sat halfway up the dugout steps. I was not able to shoot because I was shot through the hand, but the other officer, who was only shot through the leg, was able to shoot, so he lay at the top of the steps looking down the trench both ways, shooting the Germans as they came around the corners. The men down below loaded the rifle, handed it up to me and I handed it up to him.

It seemed a very long time before anything happened but just as our ammunition was running out, some English troops came down the trench from our left and they said, 'Oh, what are you doing here?' We tried to explain but they said that there were no Germans within miles. I told them that the Germans were just around the corner but they wouldn't believe me, and they turned the corner and I heard the crash of bombs. Me and my men ran the other way. What happened to the other people, I don't know. We went back to our own lines. The rest of the battalion who had followed me over the top at the beginning were all casualties. The few men I had got left were all that was left of the entire battalion.

Lieutenant Philip Howe, 10th West Yorkshires

The 10th had been so badly hit that their War Diary entry for 1 July is short and to the point:

O. A. S. [On Active Service]
At 7.30 a.m. the Battn took part in the grand assault. On the right were the 7th Divn & on the left the 21st Divn. The Battn assaulted in 4 lines. 2 lines got through the German position to the 4th line & were cut off, the attack on our left having failed. Casualties were very heavy chiefly caused by machine guns which enfiladed our left flanks & were so deadly that the 3rd and 4th lines failed to get across 'no mans land'. 27 officer casualties including Col. Dixon [commanding] & Major J. Knott 2nd in command both killed & approximately 750 O[ther] . [anks]. The Battn was then withdrawn to Ville.

War Diary 10th, West Yorkshires

Recruiting from the area around Leeds and Harrogate, the 10th Battalion of the West Yorkshire Regiment had the unenviable distinction of suffering the heaviest casualties of all the British units involved on that fateful day. When Lieutenant Howe's group and the stragglers returned, they found the battalion had been destroyed with 90 per cent of its men hit. In all, 306 men had been killed outright, with a further 404 listed as wounded or missing. A further thirty-seven men succumbed to their wounds in the days following the battle.

If the village of Fricourt fell, then men of the 7th Battalion, Alexandra, Princess of Wales' Own (Yorkshire Regiment), better known as the Green Howards, were to push forward and occupy it. If not, they were to attack it later in the day.

Owing to an unfortunate mistake on the part of the Officer Commanding 'A' Company, his company assaulted at 7.45am. As soon as they began to climb over our parapet terrific machine-gun fire was opened up by the enemy and the company was almost at once wiped out. The survivors lay in crump holes some 25 yards in front of our wire until after dark ... At 2 p.m. 1/7/16 our Artillery began the ½ hour preliminary bombardment of FRICOURT VILLAGE. This bombardment was feeble and did little damage to the enemy as the

Battalion soon learned to its cost. At 2.30 p.m. the Battn assaulted and were met by a murderous machine-gun and rifle fire, officers and men were literally mown down and were finally brought to a standstill about half way across to the enemy's trenches. 13 officers and over 300 men became casualties in about three minutes.

War Diary, 7th Battalion, Alexandra, Princess of Wales' Own Yorkshire Regiment (The Green Howards)

I got a message to say that 'A' Company on the right had assaulted … I did not believe this but sent the adjutant to find out. He reported that it was true. I could only account for this by supposing that the company commander had gone mad. Later a report came in saying that what was left of the company were lying out in front of our wire and that they were being heavily fired on by machine-guns and snipers.

Lieutenant Colonel R. Fife, 7th Green Howards

'A' Company of the 7th Green Howards had attacked with 140 men: 108 were killed or wounded within minutes.

Just north of Fricourt, 'B' Company of the 10th Green Howards followed Major Stewart Loudon-Shand over the top at Zero Hour and ran into a hail of machine gun fire.

When his company attempted to climb over the parapet to attack the enemy's trenches, they were met by very fierce machine gun fire which temporarily stopped their progress. Maj. Loudon-Shand immediately leapt onto the parapet, helped the men over it and encouraged them in every way until he fell mortally wounded. Even then he insisted on being propped up in the trench, and went on encouraging the non-commissioned officers and men until he died.

Citation for the award of the Victoria Cross to Major Loudon-Shand, *London Gazette*, 9 September 1916

To the right of 21st Division, around 9 a.m. the Territorials of the 49th (West Riding) Division were moved up from the reserve and crossed the Ancre valley behind Thiepval Wood.

We crossed the river on a very rickety bridge. German prisoners were wading through the water, holding on to the sides of the bridge. Some of our fellows were hitting them back into the water. I was horrified at the sights – dead men floating in the water, and wounded shouting for help.

Private J. G. Dooley, 1/6th West Yorkshires

I was an officer's servant and had to go with him to a conference where the brigadier (I think) met all our officers. He informed them that we had to be at the row of apple trees in Thiepval village at 4 o'clock. Our colonel tried to point out that this was impossible at the time. The answer was, 'Those are the orders'. We moved off, got into the first communication trench and found it full of prisoners. We turfed them out and proceeded towards the front line.

Private E. T. Radband, 1/5th West Yorkshires

We went forward in single file, through a gap in what had once been a hedge; only one man could get through at a time. The Germans had a machine-gun trained on the gap and when it came to my turn I paused. The machine-gun stopped and, thinking his belt had run out, or he had jammed, I moved through, but what I saw when I got to the other side shook me to pieces. There was a trench running parallel with the hedge which was full to the top with the men who had gone before me. They were all either dead or dying.

Private J. Wilson, 1/6th West Yorkshires

Every man in 2Lt Hickson's platoon of 'C' Company advanced, but after a few dozen yards he looked around and could not see a soul.

Captain E. V. Tempest. History of the 1/6th,
West Yorkshire Regiment

We saw the survivors of a kilted battalion returning down an enemy communication trench. Then they spread out in what is called Extended Order as though they were on a barrack square. The officer or NCO in charge rose and held up his arm. On his signal they all set off at a trot in perfect line towards our trenches. Within seconds, a German machine-gun was traversing them until the last man fell. I remember standing on the fire-step and screaming 'Bastards! Bastards! Bastards!' That was a word I never used.

Private W. E. Aust, Hull Commercials

After lunch we again rode up to the hill to do the 'look-see' but it was difficult to see what was happening. On returning at about 3.30 p.m. I got an order to report to the Staff Captain at Old Brigade Headquarters, Meaulte, at once, bringing with me four other officers. I ordered Keay, Kingston, Shepherd and Hart (Lt. Basil Hart, a lifelong friend; later Sir Basil Liddell Hart…) to get ready and come with me. We set off about 4.15 p.m. accompanied by Stancliffe and O'Connell, my servant and Hart's. The afternoon was very hot and dusty, and the walk from Ville to Meaulte, a distance of three miles or so, was very trying. Fortunately a horse ambulance caught us up halfway and took us to the dressing station outside Ville. Here there were large numbers of slightly wounded men, walking cases who had been dressed and were waiting to be sent away in lorries. We then reported to Capt. Buckley, who said things were going well as a whole, that our losses had been heavy and fresh officers were needed. We were to report at once to Brigade Headquarters in the trenches. We set off again. It was now 5.15 p.m. It was a long and weary walk up to the trenches, and took an endless time. It was 7.30 p.m. by the time we reported at Brigade Headquarters. The Battalion we learnt was in the Sunken Road and Crucifix Trench. The Brigadier, who looked worn and tired, told me to go up to Sunken Road at once. I was then to endeavor to reorganise the battalion – he did not seem to think there would be any other officers about, and that I should have to take charge.

Herron came and showed us the way out of the Russian Sap [a narrow communication trench]. At that moment, the Hun, no doubt realising the importance of my arrival, proceeded to put up a barrage on his own front line and no man's land. It seemed to me that discretion was the better part of valour and that I should be more useful if I made certain of getting to my destination by 9 p.m. rather than endeavor to get there by 8.30 and getting scuppered on the way … As we got out of the sap and started to go forward, a sniper started to annoy us, and progress had to be made cautiously. Each time that we got up to go forward, we would hear cries of help from wounded men who were lying all round. It may seem cruel, but it was impossible for us to pay any attention to their cries, as if we had once started 'doing doctor' to them we should never have got on at all. I therefore ordered the party not to take any notice of them, even though it seemed hard and callous, as there was more important work on hand. The sniper was most persistent all the way and very nearly winged one or two of us. At one moment I thought I saw him – he was firing from the direction of the Sausage Redoubt and I got ready to fire at him when he next showed himself. But then I noticed that there were several other men moving about near there, and as I did not know exactly where our men were, I was afraid of shooting for fear I might hit them. We finally reached the front line trench and … hurried on and finally arrived at the end of the trench where they were digging a small sap on to the road. One had to jump out and run on to the road. The man who was digging there warned us to be careful as there was a sniper, evidently in Fricourt Farm, who could see anyone getting out, and have a shot at them. I therefore made all ready to get out, and then hurriedly scrambled up and dived across the road. Sure enough I heard the 'ping' of a bullet behind me – but I was safe under the embankment on the far side of the road. Once seated there, it was distinctly amusing to watch the anxious efforts of others to get out and across safely. One member of the party in particular got so tied up in his efforts that he turned a complete

THE WAR.

GLORIOUS BRITISH ADVANCE.

WILD LOCAL RUMOURS.

Up to the hour of going to press the British continue their gloriously successful " push " in France, begun well over a week ago, and reported at length on another page.

All sorts of wild rumours were yesterday current locally concerning the Barnsley Battalions, and whilst we are not in a position to give them the lie direct, we can authoritatively say that no official news has come through which would in any way corroborate the startling tales afloat regarding the fate of our local lads.

Last night's post brought us several postcards briefly recording the fact that some of the members of the Battalions have been wounded and were—at the time of writing—being treated in the dressing stations behind the firing line, but the stories of officers and men being killed in great numbers is unsubstantiated.

During next week—should any news come through regarding the Barnsley Battalions—we shall post the messages on the front windows of the "Chronicle" Buildings. In the event of no messages being posted it must, therefore, be taken for granted that nothing of outstanding importance has transpired.

Barnsley Chronicle reports the battle.

somersault across the road, and landed on his back with his feet almost in the air under the embankment. We then proceeded north up the Sunken Road, which was simply full of men. Once we had got into the German lines, the place had seemed full of English troops, which was distinctly comforting, as on the other side it had seemed uncommonly deserted everywhere. Walking up the Sunken Road, it was necessary to keep to one side or the other, as there was a sniper who was very busy up the centre of the road. When we had gone some way up this road, I came across C. S. M. Warren, who was busy digging himself in on the side of the bank. The road here had steep sides about 12 to 15 feet high. I asked C. S. M. Warren if there were any other officers about. He did not seem to know of any, and I therefore told him that unless he found any other officers senior to me, I should be in command.

Lieutenant Lancelot Spicer, 9th KOYLI

And so, at dusk, we moved down the remnants of the trench to the front line. The last hundred yards was solid with men killed while waiting to go over. It was impossible to do other than walk on these bodies and I finally reached a man on a stretcher, with a bearer lying dead at each end. I raised my foot to place it on the chest of the man on the stretcher, when, to my amazement, he popped his head up and said quietly, 'Mind my leg, chum', and then just laid back again.

Private W. E. Aust, Hull Commercials

Those survivors still on their feet were withdrawn that night back to the billets they had left only the night before:

Arrived in dark. Had a good night's rest, many a tear shed … many spent a restless night with shaken nerves. Day's rest, all parcels and letters of missing were shared out to remainder which caused most depressing sights.

Private Charles Pickworth, 16th West Yorkshires

What a job of work clearing up the trenches was! A ghastly task having to clear the dead, poor blokes. It took days to carry them back up to Red Cottage which was an aid station. Close by mass graves had been dug prior to the battle. There wasn't enough space for the amount of dead which had to be buried so we had to use some old trenches.

Private D. C. Cameron, Sheffield Pals

Someone had seen Major Guest fall but didn't know if he had been hit and wounded or hit and killed. They decided to go out and find him that night. There were about four or five of them. They went out but they never came back.

Private Harry Hall, Barnsley Pals

I was working with the clearing up parties, you know we had a lot to do. First priority were the wounded who had to be carried up to the aid station at Red Cottage. I came across [Acting Company Sergeant Major] Atkinson who had been wounded in the chest. He was still breathing so I stripped his equipment from him, put him over my shoulder and carried him to the aid station. After much huffing and puffing I finally made it. The doctor took one look at my charge and said, 'Put him over there with the others, you've wasted your time lad, he's had it'. The sequel to this story is that some years later I became a member of Abbeydale Golf Club and in conversation with the club professional I mentioned that I had served with the City Battalion. He said his brother had also served in it and told me his name, it was CSM Atkinson. I then told him I had left him for dead at the aid station. Apparently his brother had been brought back to York where he lived until 9 July.

Private H. Hall, Sheffield Pals

Among the 7,000 men of 31st Division sent into the attack at Serre, 4,000 were killed, wounded or missing by the end of that day. The Pals battalions, recruited from tight-knit local communities had been decimated. In each battalion, a number of men were detailed off to act as 'carriers', following behind the attacking force with supplies and equipment. Others – cooks, storemen, stretcher bearers and signallers – would remain behind because their job required them to work around the battalion headquarters. It was also expected that around 10 per cent of men would be held back to form the nucleus of a new battalion if things went wrong. So, of a battalion of around 1,000 men, between 700–800 would actually take part in the assault. Six Yorkshire-based battalions reported casualties among their attacking force of at least 500. Many, of course, were slightly wounded and would, in time, return to their units, but the first day of the Somme marked the end of the Pals Battalions.

We were two years in the making and ten minutes in the destroying.

Private Arthur Pearson, Leeds Pals

Back home, news of the 'great advance' was greeted with enthusiasm:

The preliminary British bombardment paved the way to the great success afterward achieved, for it not only wrecked the enemy's first line trenches, but the second and third line defences also suffered severely. The British left nothing to chance … Serre and Montauban, two important tactical points were soon captured, and comparatively early in the fight even more valuable positions were taken after a sharp struggle. The initial success of defeating the enemy on a sixteen mile front has naturally elated the whole British Army and nation, and aroused the utmost confidence of further triumphs … With the triumphant British advance the great conflict seems entering upon its penultimate and most momentous phase.

Barnsley Chronicle, 8 July

THE WAR: GLORIOUS BRITISH ADVANCE
Wild Local Rumours

Up to the hour of going to press the British continue their gloriously successful 'push' in France, begun well over a week ago, and reported at length on another page.

All sorts of wild rumours were yesterday current locally concerning the Barnsley Battalions and while we are not in a position to give them the lie direct, we can authoritatively say that no official news has come through which would in any way corroborate the startling tales afloat regarding the fate of our lads … During next week – should any news come through regarding the Barnsley Battalions – we shall post the messages on the front window of the *Chronicle* buildings. In the event of no messages being posted it must, therefore, be taken for granted that nothing of outstanding importance has happened.

Barnsley Chronicle, 8 July

Gradually, the story began to emerge and local newspapers filled with page after page of obituaries as news filtered back. Families sought news from any source:

The relatives of the appended names of soldiers who are missing would gladly welcome any news concerning them. Will comrades in the respective regiments who have survived and are able to communicate by letter, please do so at once. No charge is made for the insertion in the *Chronicle* of particulars relative to the missing soldiers.

Barnsley Chronicle, 12 August

WALKER, Private H. 42 Kingswood Street, Great Horton, of the 2nd Bradford Pals has been reported wounded, but no letter has been received from him since July 1 and any news regarding him would be greatly welcomed by his parents. Private Walker is seventeen years of age and enlisted in April 1915. He was prior to the war, a scholar at the Wesley Place Sunday School, Great Horton and was employed by Messrs Aykroyd and Grandage Ltd.

Bradford Daily Telegraph, 22 July

In 1994 an identity disc for 19559 Private Harry Walker was found in a newly ploughed field near Serre. His body was never formally identified and today he is remembered on the Thiepval Memorial to the missing.

It was a harrowing time for me with the mothers of my friends asking for information about their sons. When I told them they had been killed or were missing they wouldn't believe me. In fact in some cases it cost friendships.

Private Douglas Cattell, Sheffield Pals

For months the vicarage almost assumed the character of a public office, for the giving of advice and the witnessing of signatures to forms by dependents and relations of soldiers and sailors. Some days visitors numbered from ten to twenty. Intermixed with much that was pathetic and sad, there were at times touches of the humorous. For example, the wife of a fallen soldier brought her five little children. It was my duty to witness her signature and to testify that I had seen the children, and that they were alive, of which there was ample evidence. Shortly afterwards came the mother of a sailor who had perished in the waters, the testatrix of his will. She brought with her two householders to testify that her statement was true. I had to seal the testimony of the three. But that was not all; evidence of identification was required, and I had to state her height, the colour of her eyes and hair, the tone of her complexion, and 'any observable peculiarity of person'. It has been of deep interest to find how many of the fallen I baptized and married. Said a mother who had lost her son: 'You married me, you baptized my four children, buried two, and married the one now killed'. Another to whom I had given a memorial card said: 'This is the third kindness you have done – you married me; you baptized my boy, and now you have given me this'. Again and again in visiting the bereaved, sorrowing, and anxious, I have been deeply touched, and oft-times it has been difficult to find words of comfort and consolation.

Revd W. Odom, Heeley, Sheffield

A week after the attack, Florence Iles wrote to her brother from their Leeds home:

My Dear Horace, I am so glad you are alright so far but I need not tell you what an anxious time I am having on your account, you have dropped in the thick of it and no mistake. I only hope you have the good luck to come back safely … we did hear that they were fetching all back from France under 19. For Goodness sake Horace tell them how old you are. I am sure they will send you back if they

Pte Horace Iles,
sixteen-year old Leeds Pal,
killed 1 July 1916.

know you are only 16, you have seen quite enough now, just chuck it up and try to get back you won't fare no worse for it. If you don't do it now you will come back in bits and we want the whole of you. I don't suppose you can do any letter writing now but just remember that I am always thinking of you and hoping for your safe return … Your loving sister Florrie.

Florrie Iles to her brother Horace,
serving in Leeds Pals, Letter dated 9 July

The letter, like many thousands sent that week, was returned to the sender. Horace lay alongside so many of his mates somewhere in no man's land on the gentle slope leading up to Serre.

Even as families at home struggled to come to terms with their grief, the war was claiming ever more victims. Day by day and week by week, the casualty lists grew longer but for the first time in living memory, the names were not just those of fighting men. This was a new sort of war, a war that reached far beyond the battlefields of France and Flanders. The shelling of Scarborough had dragged the British public into a Home Front.

On the night of 6/7 June 1915, a Zeppelin airship, designated the L9, had crossed the Yorkshire coast near Holderness and in just thirteen minutes unleashed bombs on the city of Hull that left twenty-four people dead and forty injured. Censors prohibited the reporting of raids claiming that German intelligence could gather useful information that would help them in the future. As a result, the *Hull Daily Mail* carried no direct references to the attack, although that something had happened is clear from close reading of the papers over the following week:

Preaching at St Jude's South Kensington yesterday morning, the Bishop of London said; 'When people speak of the danger to London from Zeppelins they should thank God they are allowed to have a bit of danger. We do not want to leave all the danger for the boys in the firing line. Thank God we are allowed the honour of a little danger and I shall be ashamed of London if we do not face our little bit of danger with absolutely unshaken nerves.' Those who live in districts which have the misfortune to be visited by Zeppelins will not be very ready to re-echo the cheery views of the Bishop of London when he says 'Thank God for Zeppelins' but we all know what the Bishop means ... we suppose that the Bishop has in mind those persons who do not have it in mind that a war is going on unless it is in their own backyard.

Hull Daily Mail, 7 June 1915

Schoolchildren being taught air raid drills 1915.

Zeppelin Raids – Bomb Proof Shelter. Use for one year, one person £5. F. Singleton & Co. 3 Alfred Gelder St Hull'.

'Wanted Ad', Hull Daily Mail, 9 June 1915

There was anger in the city that there were no real defences against air attack and only a dummy wooden gun guarded by a single soldier mounted on the roof of the Rose, Down & Thompson munitions factory. Public fury spilled over into an attack on a Royal Flying Corps truck and stones thrown at an RFC officer in Beverley. Determined to provide their own defence, the suggestion was made that local men should form their own flying corps. Since civilian aircraft were rarely fitted with weapons, it attracted a very special kind of volunteer:

Sir,

Having noticed in your paper a proposal to form a Corps of Aviators I would say I should be pleased to give my services and further would volunteer to act with any pilot for the purposes of a deliberate ramming of any Zeppelin or the dropping of bombs on the same at any time. I am Sir etc Joseph Noble 127 Lannaeus Street Anlaby Road Hull.

Letter to Hull Daily Mail, 11 June 1915

In August it was Goole's turn to be hit:

Goole, Aug. 12th 1915

My child,

…Mum did not wish to spoil your outing, and so did not mention anything to you to cause anxiety..'We did not expect anything would be allowed in the papers so soon by the censor. Enjoy your holiday, while you have the opportunity. Well, now! The zeps came at 11. 50 p.m. Monday. Hook bridge got the first. They tried hard for bridge, dropping 3 bombs, but all missed – they are all at the bottom of the Ouse … One fell on Jessie's back, onto the Kelsey's garden; that didn't explode, luckily; the next struck a house in Axholme street, passing thro' roof and I can tell you the deep booming roar woke me, and our room was one red glare – all Shuffelton seemed to be ablaze. Ma thought it was thunder and lightning. I kept quite cool and resigned – it was an incendiary bomb, but the fire was put out. The next fell thro roof of Mrs Acast, the stone house, next to our butcher's – four were sat at supper and three were killed; Mrs + 2 daughters, a visitor escaping … Then came some demons. One fell in George Street – 3 houses had wall blown out into the lane, and beds, bairns, bolsters and pictures after them. 4 killed … Pa, Ma, 2 children – Mr Gunnee carried girl out, all flesh of one leg torn away

- next he fetched a young baby, but the sight finished him; he was done ... sick ... he went away ... to vomit. Had it been a man, he says he would not care ... you should have seen the fugitives fleeing. Mount Pleasant was swarming; swarming. The Harrison girls slept on the bare ground, there. See a barefoot woman, only nightdress on, a baby in her arms and two children pulling at her ... 20th century culture and all up the knees in wet and field soil. We had had down pour all morning. Airmyn and Rawcliffe roads were alive, all night. All flocked out, too, on Tuesday, at dusk, but better prepared. Men and women, bairns and baskets, chairs and stools; aye and even beds were taken out to field and hedge side, road and lane, seeking safety. 14 were killed but 2 more children, girls, died in the hospital, y'day. Inquest is on this morning: funeral tomorrow. There are some 36 unexploded bombs at Police station, I am told and are to be on view this afternoon ... It would seem Mrs Acaster's visitor was hurt, and is since dead. That brings it to 17 victims; she was from London, and a relative of Mrs Ramsay's and had gone to the Acaster's for the night, so she had just walked into it, showing that we know not what a day may bring forth – what is to be, will be. Mrs Acaster is to be buried today; the rest tomorrow in common grave; Compton Rickett takes the expense ... Invite your friend to Goole, we can make her welcome; mother will be pleased to see her...

Mr West, Letter to his daughter, in Leeds

On Sunday 5/6 March 1916, the Zeppelins returned to Hull for what became known as the 'Snowy Night Raid'. One, the L14, approached Hull from the north and started dropping bombs – twenty-one explosives and two incendiaries fell in the Anlaby Road area. Another, the L11, dropped her first bomb in the Humber as it flew toward the city centre. Four people died when high explosive bombs hit Queen Street. Stained glass was shattered on the south side of Holy Trinity church. The glass roof of Paragon station was blown out. In all seventeen people died in the raid. After much lobbying, mobile anti-aircraft guns arrived ten days later and were in action on the night of 8/9 August when the L24 carried out what became known as the Selby Street Raid in which nine people died and over twenty were wounded.

It was about two in the morning when we heard windows rattling and some bombing. Then there was a lull and I wanted to just slip out to the toilet. And in that way that mothers have, I don't know – it's instilled in most mothers, in a sense she saved my life. Because as I walked out my mother unknown to me followed me, caught me up at the kitchen and said, 'Where are you going?' I said, 'Across to the toilet'. She said, 'Well I'm frightened of you putting that light on, slip out here into the garden'. So I went, opened the door on the left – she was behind me – and as I looked up, there was a light and this Zeppelin was coming up at a fast speed with quite a noisy engine. And I turned into my mother's skirt and she immediately understood what was happening. And we dashed back through the double door and were thrown across the kitchen, up the step, got level with the stairs when everything fell at the back of us. The bomb had landed about three or four yards yon side of the toilet in the garden.

Walter Doughty, Hull Schoolboy

The night of 25/26 September added Sheffield to the list of targets.

Well when we'd got up and gone out, there were very soon crowds of people coming up road and they'd got all sorts of tales about it. Sheffield was all afire and what damage they'd done. Well they didn't know, they just simply fled, sort of stampeded, into country that were just beyond us, fields. And I always remember going to have a look there, first field we got to was solid up with people on rugs and bedding on floor. But if they'd dropped a bomb on there, they'd have killed hundreds because they were so – they'd no idea what to do or how to behave and treat it.

Harry Smith, Sheffield

The Defence of the Realm Act had been strengthened to include flying kites and whistling for taxis – anything that might help guide the Zeppelins to their targets but the fact was, the airships rarely knew where they really were. After the Sheffield raid the commander reported a successful attack on Lincoln while his colleague that night, having bombed Bolton, reported having hit Derby. Some sense of the random nature of Zeppelin attacks comes from the attack of 27 November 1916 when Zeppelin LZ61, under the command of Kurt Frankenburg, crossed the coast over Atwick on Holderness as part of a nine ship attack. As it headed inland, LZ61 reached Pontefract:

In all its long history the town which has borne the shocks and blows enough had not hitherto been the object of attention of these modern murder machines, the Zepp, although more than once like engines have passed over the old Borough elsewhere on wicked slaughter bent, so that Monday nights visitation was at once a novel and altogether alarming experience. The first intimation of the presence of Zepps in the district was assumed when the public gas supply was turned very low at about 9.15 p.m. At about 10.30 the doubts of most people were determined by the distant booms of bursting bombs. Then of course everybody began to be interested. Meantime the 'specials' [special constables] were discharging their duty in a way that does them exceeding credit. At this time it was thought that the effort of destruction was aimed at distant munition works or at some large centre of population, but when at about 11 o'clock there were terrific explosions and loud reports accompanied by heavy gun shooting none needed to be told that at last the Huns were upon them. As a matter of fact, proved next morning by many witnesses, one or more of the terrible visitants hovered over the town and the neighbourhood for a considerable time, dealing out, had they been accurately aimed, sufficient bombs to destroy half the town and many of the dwellers therein, not to speak of several big villages at some distance … It was at this time that the effects of the explosions and the shooting were most telling making the windows of old properties rattle, smashing some, and rousing the townsfolk, the people of the countryside, and the villagers generally. There is no need to say that many persons were scared, that many remained calm and cool, and that a large number of people risked going into the open to see the unwanted sight – a raider airship hovering, droning, throbbing with inward forces and threatening everybody and everything beneath it … About 11 o'clock the shooting and bombing explosions, near or distant, became less frequent and shortly afterwards the droning gradually died away in the distance. Those who had taken refuge in basements etc came out to learn what could be learnt and others retired to their beds. The visitation was not ended however for at about 11.30 the unwelcome sound of distant bombs was heard and in an amazingly short time bombs exploded quite near and the droning was again practically overhead accompanied by what sounded like cracks of 'heavens artillery' terrific and nerve shaking to quiet peaceable people. The experience however did not last long and about 11.45 the visitors cleared off for good although explosions were heard in the distance, either of their making or the shots of airmen in pursuit. For the space of an hour or more there were many people in the streets curious to see all and learn all they might and some, especially where children were concerned, remained in what they thought to be safe places. Upon the whole it may be said that the townsfolk behaved bravely and that the 'specials' did their duty as brave folk would expect them to do it. Next morning was given up by large numbers of people to investigation and gossip in regard to the visitation. Many persons without a doubt saw the Zepp, possibly two … That thousands of people on Tuesday and Wednesday and since have inspected these evidences of the nocturnal visit needs scarcely be stated. Hundreds have carried off souvenirs of the occasion in the form of bits of shrapnel etc. The prevailing feeling is astonishment – that the town should be thought worthy of attention and that so marvellous an escape from harm has been the townsfolk's portion. As regards certain villages not far distant we find that eleven or twelve bombs of both kinds were dropped. Five explosions fell into waste heaps, two

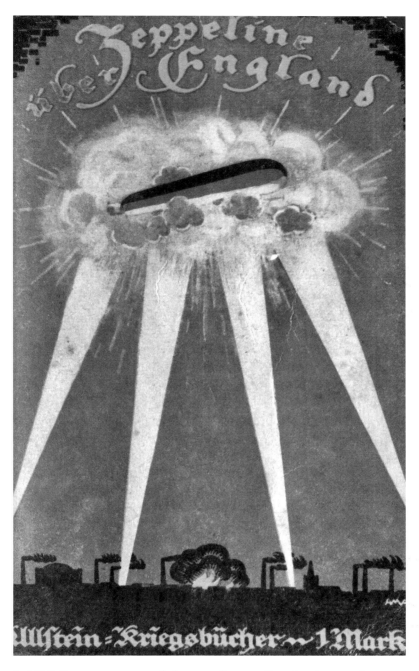

A 1916 German account of the zeppelin war lists the dates and targets of raids. Comparing these with reports of towns actually hit shows that zeppelin crews were frequently lost as they flew over Britain.

incendiaries struck the ground close to an old residence, an incendiary which did not explode found its billet in a field and three incendiaries dived into an immense waste pile. In no instance was any damage of note done, no building was struck, and no person was seriously injured. Marvellous is the only word that fits the circumstances … On Thursday afternoon an inquest was held … on the body of a woman who died from shock during the raid. The woman who was forty-nine years of age had for some time past been suffering from heart trouble, for which she had been attended by a doctor. When the alarm was given on Monday night she along with other women and some children sought safety in a cellar in a garden near her home. She got over the shock of the first visit all right but when on the return journey an airship dropped an explosive bomb within 300 yards of her home she fainted and died in the arms of a neighbour a few minutes later. Although bombs were dropping all round the countryside, the deceased's daughter bravely set out on her cycle through very lonely country to fetch a doctor, but her mother had passed away before the doctor arrived. The coroner expressed his deep sympathy with the husband and family and later in summing up the evidence, said that the poor woman's death was directly due to the murderous barbarity of the enemy, that it was a disgusting and cruel shame. The jury unanimously returned the following verdict: Died from shock due to fright owing to bombs dropped by an enemy airship near her home.

Pontefract and Castleford Express, 1 December 1916

Another occasion when a Zeppelin airship came anywhere near Leeds – the night of Monday, November 27, 1916 – its presence was made known by the sound of bombs dropped indiscriminately in Pontefract Park, twelve miles away, and the dull boom of the explosions was heard plainly on the north side of Leeds. The warning [was] given to the city … and many people spending the evening in town had scarcely reached their homes on the outskirts when, just at the hour of midnight, the explosions broke the silence of the night. It was not known until next day – and then only through gossip locally – that the alarm was caused by two Zeppelins which had been careering around the Barnsley district and were making their way back to the coast. One airship went off in the direction of Ferrybridge, and the other in a more northerly direction, passing over the V[oluntary] A[id] D[etachment] hospital at Ledstone Hall, and creating a diversion for the convalescent soldiers, many of whom turned out of bed to see all that was to be seen … 'We can never, of course, know what was in the mind of the officer in charge of the bomb dropping gear', wrote a Yorkshire Post correspondent afterwards. 'He may have thought that he was over some of the big works of Leeds – only about ten miles away – or he may merely have been in a hurry to finish his work and get home to breakfast. At any rate, in quick succession he rained incendiary bombs upon the unoffending turf of Harewood Park; and when day broke most of these were pulled up out of the damp soil like ripe turnips and formed a most interesting exhibition in the coach-house of the Harewood Arms. At the time, it was suggested that the commander of the Zeppelin knew more than he was generally credited with, and that in dropping these bombs he was merely endeavouring to carry out the principles of Applied Kultur, Harewood House being then in use as a Red Cross Hospital. The Germans probably knew that it was not defended by anti-aircraft guns, as were the arsenals of Leeds.' Having successfully disturbed the turf in the Park, and, by then, having only a few more bombs left, the raider turned eastwards for home. He may or may not have been able to see the houses of the hamlet. At any rate, as he was crossing the main road near to the principal gates of the Park, he dropped another incendiary bomb. This fell on the corner of the roof of a cottage, but with such ill-luck from the enemy's point of view that on going through the tiles it sank into the water cistern, and was immediately extinguished. The impact of the falling bomb destroyed the cistern and flooded the bedroom below, but such damage can hardly be said to be worth even the cost of the bomb. The Zeppelin's farewell to Harewood was another incendiary bomb which dropped into an empty hen-house belonging to Dr Matthews. Over the line of Harewood Avenue, the Zeppelin came within view of the anti-aircraft gun station between East Keswick and Collingham, was picked up by the searchlight, and was fired upon, though without result. By way of acknowledgment the Zeppelin dropped its last two incendiary bombs, both of which fell in the field in which the gun was placed. An incendiary bomb dropping into a soft, damp meadow is not a very terrifying thing, and here, again, beyond a couple of holes in the turf, the Germans achieved nothing. Perhaps the greatest things that they might claim for their enterprise were that they had dropped quite a large weight of bombs on the estate of the Lord Lieutenant, the representative of the King in the West Riding, and had avoided running any very great risk themselves. That Leeds escaped was the more remarkable because on the same night a fire broke out at the Kirby Banks Screw Works, near Meadow Lane, and although soon subdued, was at its brightest when the Zeppelin was hovering over Wharfedale. It was, indeed, the flares which had been lit in Pontefract Park, to guide our aeroplanes there, that attracted so much attention in that particular neighbourhood. The night was exceedingly still; the sky was clear and star-lit; but the darkness which had been systematised all over the city ensured protection.

William Herbert Scott

In fact, the Zeppelin was not heading away from Barnsley, but towards it:

One night that will long be remembered by the natives of Silkstone was Nov. 28th, 1916 the time of the Zeppelin raids. We had read of these raids, but no one expected them as far inland as Silkstone. I remember having gone to bed when I was awakened by the rattling of the old windows of the vicarage but thought little of it. Presently I heard a deal of talking outside and some knocking. I got up and went to the window and was told that the Zepps were near, and I could hear the boom, boom of the bombs. We all got up and went out into the garden. It was a clear night, no wind, and the stars visible, when from the distance one heard the deep purring of the powerful motor. Presently, as we watched, over Dodworth a tiny black thing appeared in the sky, every minute growing bigger as it made its way over the Fall Wood – a flash of light, a crash, a zoom, and we knew a bomb had fallen' then another. On came the aerial monster, for all the world like a huge cigar, until it appeared to be directly over the church, whose leaden roof, slightly frosted, glistened in the night. There it seemed to hover, and after a minute's pause when the engines were quiet, turned a half left turn and made off for the Common. We were crouching in the vicarage garden and the Zepp was moving slowly and at a low altitude, and its two cars were quite visible to me. No words can express our sense of relief when the monster veered away. In the village the panic was universal and people sought shelter in the old disused day-holes and elsewhere. The men in the camp had scattered. No bombs were actually dropped at Silkstone, but three at Dodworth, one exploding on the pit-heap at Church Lane collieries. I saw two unexploded ones the next day in the camp and they were death-dealing-looking-things. No one was killed, and it is probable the burning slag-heaps of Church Lane collieries attracted the Zepp. It hovered over Barnsley Workhouse a long time, nd from the slow way in which it was moving led one to suppose it was crippled and had possibly lost its way. It may have been the one which in that raid perished off the Norfolk coast. Though we at other times heard the bombs we never had another unpleasant visitor so near.

Revd Joseph Prince, Silkstone

LZ61 wandered on, later bombing towns in the Potteries before turning for home. It never made it. Passing over Lowestoft, it was attacked by British fighters and crashed into the sea. There were no survivors.

In comparison to what was to come a generation later, the Zeppelin raids were little more than a nuisance, but for a nation that had believed itself to be protected by the English Channel and the might of the Royal Navy, the threat of being attacked in their own homes brought shockwaves of terror through the population. The merest hint of a Zeppelin raid brought production in factories to a halt as workers fled into the open countryside – although the German bombs fell more often into empty fields than onto real targets.

As the British Army recovered from its losses on the Somme, life on the home front was about to get even harder.

5

1917:
'SURELY WE ARE WINNING?'

By 1917, it was truly a world war.

In order to ensure that entitlement to the British War Medal and the Allied Victory Medal were recorded, a system of Medal Index Cards was later developed to record each man's service. Today, the National Archive at Kew holds a list of abbreviations used to indicate which units men might have served in, that runs to sixty-four pages, ranging from the Arab Rifles to the Bermuda Contingent of the Royal Garrison Artillery and the Burma Military Police, the Ceylon Planters Rifle Corps and on through the Libyan Arab Force, the Malay States Guides to the Zion Mule Corps. In the first week of the war the British government asked Japan, its ally since 1902, for help in destroying the German naval presence in Chinese waters. On 23 August, Japan formally declared war on Germany and two days later on Austria-Hungary, followed on 2 September by a Japanese landing at the German colony of Tsingtao. In 1916, Britain's oldest ally, Portugal, sent troops to the Western Front and the entry of the United States into the war on 6 April 1917 was followed by declarations of war on Germany by Cuba, Panama and Bolivia. On 10 April, Bulgaria declared war on the United States. Later that year, Greece, Thailand, Liberia and China all declared war on Germany and its allies. By 1918, Honduras, Brazil and Ecuador had all joined the alliance against Germany. Tiny Monaco lost a total of eight men in the war – 10 per cent of its entire expeditionary force. Few corners of the globe remained unaffected.

Soldier with his mascot, Mesopotamia.

Across Yorkshire, newspapers carried stories and letters from local men serving on all fronts. In October 1914, 1st Battalion KOYLI left Singapore for the Western Front, to be replaced by the Indian 5th Light Infantry, a Muslim battalion from Madras, but a few weeks later the Ottoman Empire declared a jihad on Britain and its allies. Millions of Muslims around the world regarded Sultan Mehmed V as their spiritual leader and the Germans, aware that nearly half the world's 270 million Muslims lived under British, French or Russian rule, encouraged rebellion. A rumour spread around Singapore that the British were arranging to send the 5th Light Infantry to fight in Turkey against Turkish Muslims, and on the afternoon of 15 February, they mutinied, killing their British officers. British, French, Russian and Japanese ships converged on the port two days later and their marines fought a fierce battle to suppress the mutineers.

Six of our Company were sent with a party from H. M. S. *CADMUS* to a place called Bukit-Panjang, a native village in the jungle, to search the native houses for mutineers. We found three under a bed in one of the dwellings, and gave them short shrift. From there we were sent to Tanglin, and found fourteen more hiding in the churchyard. We next moved to Fort Canning, to guard the signalling station, and when we left there about a fortnight later, the majority of the mutineers were accounted for.

Pte. T. E. Hughes, 10, Ernest Street, Cornholme, a member of the 4th King's Shropshire Regiment, on duty in Singapore in February 1915

Although Mahatma Gandhi would go on to become the leader of the Indian independence movement, in 1914 he had described the British as being 'in a righteous cause for the good and glory of human dignity and civilisation' and declared, 'our duty is clear: to do our best to support the British'. Hundreds of thousands of Indians volunteered to fight but not all felt the same way. Throughout the war British troops remained in India, constantly alert for signs of rebellion:

We left the Indus about noon, and it was soon obvious that we were getting nearer the frontier. We were continually passing small forts, and the natives who boarded the train at the different stations we stopped at were all armed more or less according to their means. The people who were reasonably well off were armed with rifles or guns, and were bristling with ammunition, while the poor people simply carried evil-looking axes over their shoulders. We eventually reached Bannu about eight o'clock, only four hours late. We were covered with dust, for the railway

First World War British troops in Palestine.

track was thick with sand from the desert on either side. As we could not get a conveyance to Miranshah under twenty-four hours' notice, the three of us who were going there had to wait in Bannu from Monday night till Wednesday morning ... [Miranshah] is absolutely new. The British have not been here long, and so everything is very rough. Officers are housed in half-built rooms, which are really glorified mud huts. There is a wall round the camp, with wire entanglements in front of it. The city gates' are opened at 7 a.m. and closed at 6 p.m. after which time no one is allowed out. If we go out during the day we must take an escort. British officers always go on parade with revolvers. There are only two native regiments here, each about a thousand strong, a Gurkha regiment and ourselves. We have thirteen British officers, and they have about the same, so that there are not more than thirty Britishers in the whole place. We are very close to Afghanistan – the Afghan hills are in full view only a very short distance away ... On Monday I had to take my Company out about three miles, and make an attack over three ranges of hills. They were 200 strong, each armed with rifle and 100 rounds of ammunition, myself with a fully loaded revolver, and not a single man with me who could speak or understand a word of English, in a country known to be hostile. Everything went off all right, and I quite enjoyed it.

Lieutenant Alfred King, of Gaudy Bridge, writing from Mud Flats,
Miranshah on the Afghan frontier

In 1914, the modern day East African states of Tanzania, Zambia, Mozambique, Rwanda, Burundi, Kenya, Uganda and the Democratic Republic of Congo were all under the control of European powers. Sporadic fighting broke out along the borders of German and British East Africa around Mount Kilimanjaro and a British amphibious assault was launched to capture the vital port town of Tanga but in the middle of the battle, swarms of bees disturbed by the noise launched their own offensive, sending both forces running. Under orders to divert men and resources away from Europe, the German commander Lettow-Vorbeck fought a cat-and-mouse guerilla campaign that over the next four years would involve nearly 400,000 Allied soldiers, sailors, merchant marine crews, builders, bureaucrats, and support personnel in the East Africa campaign, assisted in the field by an additional 600,000 African bearers.

I was in a troop train on a 300-mile thirty-six hour journey inland. During the day we saw from the train, roaming quite free, ostriches, giraffes, zebras, and any amount of buck, ranging from wee delicate looking specimens to animals with horns two to three feet long. A month later we were camped near the railhead, quite out in the wilderness. Some of our camping places have been far from ideal. One which we stayed at three weeks was under the slopes of Mount Kilimanjaro (19,000 feet high), with his perpetual cap of snow. At times the mountain is a wonderful sight. It is said that the natives worship it, and I for one don't wonder. You would be highly amused to see the rig-outs of some of the natives. For general simplicity, a light blanket draped over one shoulder takes some beating. As further adornment he may have a piece of cane fixed in the lobe of each ear, several coils of copper wire round his neck, half a dozen brass rings round each wrist, and a similar number of iron ones round the ankles. The general result is a sort a walking junk shop. Others of them go in rather more for style, and pick up all the cast-off clothing they can find, either civilian or military. I saw one stalking along the other day dressed in a waist-cloth and a morning coat, smoking a pipe with a cane bowl and a long iron stem ... I have not seen much in the way of big game, but at the other extreme I have seen enough different sorts of crawling, jumping and flying insects to last me the rest of my natural existence.

Pte. Wilfred Ormerod, of Cornholme, serving with the Motor Transport Section in East Africa, writing home in August, 1916

The compartments were worse than the 'Paddy's Mail', no windows, doors missing, and compartments about three-quarters the size of those in England. Seven of us, with our kit, were in each, and it was not so bad until it came to sleeping, and then the fun started. Three on the floor, one under each seat and two on the seat was the arrangement and it was a marvel how we managed to get off to sleep. We passed many stations, and had fun with the blacks. At one station about nine p.m. One chap wanted us to pay six cents for two bananas. This was too much, so one chap kicked the basket in the air. Just outside another station we had a game of football, and although the weather was terribly hot it was a great treat to us. Most of the journey was through the jungle, and the foliage and scenery were lovely. We saw giraffes, wild boars, ostriches, deer parrots and wild cats and although we saw no monkeys we heard enough of them at night-time when we wanted to get off to sleep. It was a journey I shall never forget. We fed on bully and biscuits all the while and each man brewed his own tea with water from the engine boiler. We are now in camp about 6,000 feet above the sea level and although it is hot during the day it gets very cold at night. Tobacco is a shilling a pound and good fags can be had at ten a penny, so you needn't trouble about sending parcels.

Private A. Williamson, Hoyland, Barnsley

Egypt and control of the Suez Canal remained vital to the passage of ships to and from India and Australia and provided the base for operations in the Middle East. Ottoman forces threatened oil fields around Basra and the British, with support from Arab leaders keen to rid themselves of centuries of Ottoman control, fought not only the Turks, but extremes of temperature that regularly soared above 120°F in the arid deserts interspersed with regular flooding; flies, mosquitoes and other vermin that all led to appalling levels of sickness and death through disease. Medical support was poor, with wounded men spending up to two weeks on boats before reaching any kind of hospital. 11,000 men were killed in action and another 4,000 died of wounds, but over 12,000 died of illnesses and over 13,000 were listed as missing or prisoners.

Dear Mother, I expect you are anxiously awaiting this letter, but this will relieve you a bit. I have been sent from my regiment to Bombay in India. I expect to be getting on a boat for England any time now. Bombay is such a grand place I feel as though I don't want to leave it, but again I would rather be at home; it would be all right if you lived here. When I left the regiment we were halfway between Kut-el-Amara and Baghdad. I was in all the fighting for Kut, and it was pretty warm, too. I was not sorry when I got out of it. Poor old Johnny Turk got two bombardments a day, and then as soon as the bombardments ceased we made a rush at him with bayonets and bombs. He did not wait for either. The sight of us was enough. He would take his hook, and a good job for him too. I will have plenty to tell you when I come, so cheer up – it won't be long. If I am sent to France, when I get home there will be one consolation: I shall know what to expect. So will close now, hoping you are all feeling like I am. PS – My first day in the trenches was Xmas Day.

Pte John Nettleton, Harrogate, serving with the
Mesopotamian Expeditionary Force, 1917

The prospect of marching through lands they knew from their Bibles was exciting, but the reality was very different. One unidentified soldier wrote home to Todmorden:

Since leaving England I have been on the move nearly all the time; all round Africa – Sierra Leone, Cape Town, Durban, and Zanzibar; then Mesopotamia, including Basra, Amara, Kut, Bagdad, and the Samara front, though I did not see much fighting there. Since leaving Mesopotamia we have been at the following places: Muscat, Aden, Port Suez, Ismailia, Kantara, and now we are stationed in a most beautiful village on the Palestine front. From the verandah of our bungalow we can see all sorts of fruit growing: grapes, bananas, oranges, lemons, pomegranates, apples, tomatoes; in truth it is a land flowing with milk and honey. I shall never forget passing through the place where the Garden of Eden, was supposed to be. The dust was about a foot deep, and you could not see the horse in front of you.

We were flooded out of the trenches, and got over the parados. I and three more chaps were sniping the Turks, who also were flooded out. We had been sniping about forty-five minutes when I got one in the head. I spun round like a top, and thought for a few minutes that my time had come. Then I was all right and walked to the dressing station, about three miles, up to the knees in water. We had been flooded out a week previous to that, on April 12th, and we had to retire and dig fresh trenches, while the Turks kept up heavy artillery fire, and killed and wounded several of our chaps. It is no picnic up there I can assure you. When it rains it turns the sand into mud, and you are up to the boot tops in it. When the sun comes it is terrible, 130 degrees in the shade, 150 in the sun, and all is sand again. You eat sand, breathe sand, get sand in your eyes, sand up your nose, sand in your ears, and sand in the water you drink. Then there are not only the Turks to fight, but a dozen different diseases, a few of which are dysentery, malaria, rheumatic fever, sand-fly fever, and typhoid. You sit down to eat your bread, again, and you get swarms of flies around. Your bread is black with them; you take your right hand to your mouth, and keep continually waving your left hand. If you stop you cannot see your bread for flies, and while you are doing this there will be dozens swimming in your tea. When you get down for a few hours' rest between sentry-go you are pestered with mosquitoes, and you feel you can rub and scratch yourself until you bleed.

Unidentified Cornholme soldier, 1916

After the evacuation of Gallipoli, troops remained around what is now Thessaloniki in Northern Greece on what was known as the Salonica Front. We get used to anything – sickness, disease, bullets, shells or bombs. We are like pawnbrokers, we contract to take anything on. I thought we had some hills in France, but they are only molehills. This is the place for mountains. When we were up in Serbia it took us exactly six and a half hours to get to the top of one. What a country! It is all rocks and mountains; there were no roads here until we made them. There has been some splendid work done out here. The boys have had to work very hard, road making and trench digging, under severe weather conditions. We expect big game here, but we are ready for them. It is a very ancient country, and they wear the same old-fashioned dress yet. They are very fond of colours, and oxen are used for carting purposes. We did not know whether it was Christmas or not up the line. We went trench digging as usual, and the same old bully beef and biscuits for dinner.

Private Albert J. Norton

Italy had originally been part of an alliance with Germany and Austria-Hungary, but in 1914 had argued that the alliance was a defensive one and so placed Italy under no obligation to join them in a war of aggression. Instead, after long negotiations, Italy joined the war on the allied side in 1915. British troops were sent to reinforce the Italian Front:

We had tremendous welcomes everywhere, particularly when we got into Italy. Every time we stopped we found crowds on the platforms waiting for us, and they gave us sandwiches, hot coffee, biscuits, flowers, and cigarettes; also we got big bunches of grapes and carnations. At Milan the people went pretty well mad. We had three or four hours there, and were split into parties of about fifty, and marched through the city. The streets were simply packed, and wherever we went we were pelted with flowers.

Corporal J. H. Garside, Royal Army Medical Corps,
March 1917

In the Mediterranean, the British base at Malta provided a centre for operations. Busy though life was, it had a lot of compensations:

We have cricket, football, hockey, swimming, dancing, and all kinds of sports, and in amusements we have about half a dozen picture palaces, and a fine opera house, where during the season. Italian operas are given. Malta is a very interesting place. There are some fine old buildings, built by the Knights of St John; also some beautiful churches, the interior walls and pillars of which are of marble, and ornaments of gold and silver are quite common. The religious processions, too, are wonderful. Oranges, lemons, figs, melons, grapes, and such like grow out in the open. The weather is beautiful. We get rain about every six months, but the sirocco winds are nearly as bad as rain. As in other hot climates, we get mosquitoes, whose bites are terrible, and sandflies, which cause fever. What strikes us most is the number of goats one sees here. They go about in droves, and their owners do a good trade in milk, which the Maltese people drink, but we are not allowed to drink it, as it causes Mediterranean fever. A good many of the people are very dirty, but the rest are well dressed, and it is quite a treat to go down the principal street on Saturdays and Sundays.

Private James Henry Stansfield, Royal Army Medical Corps,
Valetta Hospital in Malta, 18 October 1916

Welfare facilities at a munitions factory.

The Russian Revolution of 1917 triggered a civil war between the Red and White Russian armies that would continue after the Armistice in Europe. In late 1918, British troops were sent to assist the White forces:

I shall never forget the sight as we passed Cape Helles and 'W' Beach, where the local lads paid so heavily in the landing. The relics of the landings are still lying there in the form of the *RIVER CLYDE* and the remains of old dug-outs and trenches, and the whole thing seemed to us, as we sailed close by, as one picture of desolation. The journey through the Narrows to Constantinople was full of interest. We arrived off Constantinople as the day was breaking, and my first glimpse of the city was through a grey mist and rain, but as the day lengthened we got a splendid view of the whole place, and it was a sight worth seeing. After a stay of about three hours, we set sail again up the Bosphorus and the scenery there also was something to remember, until about five o'clock, when we headed into the Black Sea, and ran into quite heavy swells again, which kept up all night. We got our first glimpse of Batoum early in the morning, and it looked a dismal sight through the pouring rain. We are for the present billeted in some Russian barracks, and are as comfortable as lords. We are only here for a few days, and then we are going inland to Tiflis, in the Caucasus Mountains, about half-way between the Black Sea and the Caspian Sea, so we have a two days' journey before us.

Corporal Sidney Uttley, en route for Tiflis,
in the Caucasus Mountains, 1918

Meanwhile, at the other end of the country,

I wish you could have seen Archangel to-day. For two days we have had almost continued snow, and the main street is a picture. Six inches of snow, beautifully white – there are no tall chimneys to pollute the atmosphere with multitudinous blacks – frozen until it crunches musically under one's feet. The footpaths are trodden hard, and are so smooth and slippery that the small boys use skates along them, but the roads are practically untouched, except where the trams run, and the small horse sleighs pass. The people are all suitably clad to fit into the scene – the ladies with fur coats and caps, and many of the men as well; the scene beggars description. People go to market with little hand sleighs, and you can see a lady dressed in furs which would make a Bond Street lady envious, dragging a little sleigh with numerous newspaper covered parcels breaking open and showing the contents. With all the degrees of frost, though, it is not cold as we think of it at home. The river is almost full of floating ice, and we anticipate that it will be frozen over completely by the end of the month, and then motors will be running over it instead of river steamers running through it, and in another month there will be a railway on it. We have just been given the meteorological reports for the 1917–18 winter. How would you like an average fall of snow in the open country of between ten and fifteen feet, and a mean temperature in January of minus 17 degrees F?

Sergeant-Major Walter Lee, Royal Army
Medical Corps at Archangel, 19 November 1918

As the war took men to places they had barely imagined, a new world was also opening up for the families they had left behind them.

Victory in this appalling war now depends upon the women. A strange thing to say, but absolutely true … we have reached the stage when it rests with our women to see that their sons and husbands, their sweethearts and brothers, do not fight a losing battle; it is for our women to see that our dead have not died in vain; it is for our women to see that their children shall not live in a Prussian brutalised world.

Saddleworth Reporter, November 1916

German U-Boats had been given orders to attack any shipping they found and ships carrying vital supplies were being targeted. Food was becoming increasingly scarce and national rationing had to be introduced in early 1917. Local schemes had already been put in place in the West Riding:

The conduct of certain tradespeople who at this time shut their shops to the general public and sent out meat and other goods to favoured customers via the back door infuriated the people and occasionally the luckless butcher boys were held up and the contents of their basket looted. The knowledge that some well-to-do folk were hoarding food also caused discontent. It was these annoyances which made local authorities adopt rationing schemes before national compulsory rationing came into force.

Dorothy Peel

We must all eat less food, especially we must all eat less bread and none of it must be wasted. The enemy is trying to take away our daily bread. He is sinking our wheat ships. If he succeeds in starving us our soldiers will have died in vain.

Ministry of Food, 1917

I am a slice of bread. I measure three inches by two-and-a-half and my thickness is half-an-inch. My weight is exactly an ounce. I am wasted once a day by 48,000,000 people of Britain … When you throw me away or waste me you are adding twenty submarines to the German Navy.

Ministry of Food, 1917

Ration display, Keighley, 1917.

Keighley was held up by the national press as an example of patriotic frugality with its campaign to reduce food waste, public lectures on how to produce meals for 4*d* a day, and recipes for loaves made from rice, maize and pearl barley. Local schoolchildren sang 'Each Loaf Saved Drives a Big, Long Nail'. The story grew of a visitor from Barnsley who gazed in amazement at the display of a day's rations in a shop window: six small sausages, half a loaf and half a saucer of sugar. 'By Gum, we eat as much as that at Barnsley while we're waiting for dinner. If that's what they're doing at Keighley, I'm off home!'

Hoarding food became an offence under DORA and finding enough to eat became the focus of everyone's attention.

Food queues, 1917. School attendances fell as children were sent to stand in queues for whatever was available.

The most awful thing was food, it was very scarce. As we were coming off shift, someone would say, 'There is a bit of steak at the butcher's'. And I would get off the train and then go on the tram and I'd get off at Burley Road and run to the shop. Only to find a long queue and by it got to my turn there would be no more meat, only half a pound of sausage. You see, that's coming off night shifts, you went straight into a queue before you could go to bed. Then my mother would be in home needing half a stone of flour for the kids, you see. We were lucky if we got up to bed by 11 a.m. and up again at four to catch the train, five o'clock to Barnbow.

Elsie McIntyre, Leeds munitions worker

We had the ration books and we all used to stand in the queues for cigarettes, meat and what have you. If we were walking up the road and saw a queue at a shop we used to stand in it ... to see what they'd got and whatever it was we used to get some.

H. Middleton, Sheffield Boy Scout, 1917

Schools reported a growing problem with absenteeism as children we sent to wait for hours in long queues for whatever rationed items could be found.

Mum took me up there and put me in the queue and she says, 'Now stand still and don't move until I get the other ones away to school and I'll come back. But keep my place'. Of course I was standing there and the snow was deep, it was right up over your feet. The next thing I knew, I was lying on a bench in the dairy. I'd fainted.

Maud Cox, eight years old, in 1917

The prices of other staples rose sharply.

Mr Jowett asked the Parliamentary Secretary to the Ministry of Food whether he is aware that there are 303 fish friers' shops in Bradford that supply, altogether, between 800,000 and 900,000 meals per week consisting of fish and potatoes, fried, in all cases, in pure beef dripping; that these meals are provided at an average cost to the consumer of 2*d* to 2½ *d* each; if he is aware that although 4,000 stones of potatoes per week are used in providing these meals and a large proportion of the potatoes are purchased on the cooperative system by the fish friers in the city the potatoes have to be bought at retailers' prices; if he is aware that under the present arrangement in regard to prices it is becoming a general practice among potato merchants to buy from farmers, whether by reason of collusion or of necessity is not known, as if the farmers were retailers, and with the result that fish friers and others are obliged to pay extra cartage charges and commission to potato merchants over and above farmer-retailers' prices or go without supplies; and if, in view of the importance of maintaining the supply of cheap nutritious meals economically cooked and served during the present crisis, he will consent to receive a deputation of fish friers and allow them to explain their case to him?

House of Commons Debate, *Hansard*, 9 April 1917

Landlords, too, attempted to take advantage of the situation by raising rents until the Rent Restriction Act was brought in to prevent the families of men at the front being forced out into the street.

Chaplains with the troops at the front started sending me distressing letters from the wives of soldiers in their regiments, containing notices to quit ... Several wrote me stinging letters asking what these landlords were up to, as their men were beside themselves upon receipt of such letters from home and were threatening to return to England and finish off the landlords and then come back to Flanders and polish off the Germans.

Dan Rider, Housing Campaigner

Against such a background, wives and mothers attempted to keep the family together. Those who could found work in the many industries now forced to take in women. There was always a need for munitions workers where the toxic chemicals caused serious illness and even death. There was another risk, too.

At about 2.27 p.m. on Monday 21 August 1916, a labourer, named James Broughton, was moving barrels of picric acid when he heard a fizzing sound. As he turned to search for the source, he realised that flames were coming from the top of one of the barrels, he raised the alarm but the sprinkler system was broken and, around 2.45 p.m. a massive explosion ripped through the Low Moor factory, triggering smaller explosions that continued until late that evening. Windows shattered and around 2,000 homes were damaged by the concussion of the blast, fifty so seriously they had to be rebuilt. Clouds of coloured smoke drifted across the area. In 1917, the medical inspector of nearby Raw Nook School reported large numbers of children with enlarged tonsils which he attributed to exposure to the chemicals. Thirty-eight people died as a result of the explosion and the shock affected the community for years.

During the week it has been ascertained that many of the children have definitely left the district. Many others are away from home until the houses are restored. The attendance is still very poor.

'Low Moor Church of England School Logbook',
11 September 1916

February 19th. The school re-opened this morning with only ten children present…

February 26th. A few more children made an appearance today, some for the first time since last July. Still only 40 present.

'Low Moor Church of England School Logbook'

The huge munitions complex at Barnbow near Leeds employed staff from as far afield as York, Harrogate and Wakefield and needed thirty-eight trains per day just to transport its staff to and from work. By late 1916 there were 16,000 people working at Barnbow from the 130,000 who had applied for jobs there. Most were women, affectionately known as 'The Barnbow Lasses' and, like all 'munitionettes', had the yellow skin associated with working with explosives. Since milk was believed to help reduce the problem, Barnbow had a herd of 120 cows producing 300 gallons a day to supply its workforce.

Just after 10 p.m. on Tuesday 5 December 1916, several hundred women and girls had just started their shift at the factory, 170 going to

Room 42, where 4.5 inch shells were being filled, fused and prepared for delivery. At 10.27 p.m. a violent explosion suddenly rocked Room 42, killing thirty-five women outright, and maiming and injuring many more, leaving many of the dead only identifiable by the identity disks they wore around their necks. The machine where the explosion occurred was completely destroyed. Yet so vital was the work that production was stopped only for a short while, and once the bodies were removed, other girls volunteered to work in Room 42 that same night.

I came on duty early the next morning. Work was going on as normal but Room 42 was a bloodstained shambles. The accident is believed to have happened when a shell exploded as it was being fused, probably because it had been too tightly screwed down.

Arthur Peck, Horsforth

Censorship at the time prevented news of the disaster from reaching the press, the death notices reported only that they were 'killed by accident'. In the aftermath, the value of each girl's life was assessed in a neat copperplate script:

Katherine Bainbridge. Age 30. Claimant: husband age 45 – a discharged soldier. 4 children 3 boys 10, 5 and 2, and girl 7. Claimant has a pension of £1 a week until June 191 He states that deceased contributed 26/- weekly to support of household. Her average weekly wages is given as 17/5. Remarks: Partial dependency of children.

Assessment of workers killed in the Barnbow explosion.

Edith Sykes age 15¾. Claimant father aged 43, a hydraulic press hand earning 30s to 35s a week. Eight children left in family, three girls and five boys ages 21, 19, 13, 11, 9, 7, 5, 2. Total amount contributed by children £1-13-00. Deceased is said to have contributed £1-00-00, claimant from £1-10-00 to £1-15-00. Remarks: No dependency £3 on account of burial expenses has been paid. Olive Yeates age 17. Claimant father aged 43, Railway Ticket Collector earning 38/- a week. One boy aged 7 left. Deceased worked two weeks average 11/6. Remarks: No dependency. Burial expenses up to £10.

> National Archives File MUN 4/4893, 'EXPLOSIONS:
> Explosion at No. 1 National Filling Factory', Crossgates, Leeds;
> list of fatal casualties and question of compensation

Despite the danger, munitions work was highly sought after. Wages averaged £3 a week but bonuses could sometimes push this as high as £10 – a huge amount at the time that allowed women an opportunity to enjoy their leisure time. Among their newfound freedoms, women could, for the first time, afford to go out with friends rather than entertain at home. It became acceptable for them to enter pubs on their own without an escort and concerns were raised about the decline in moral standards:

There used to be a train go this way to Barnbow, a train go that way to York and half of them that come from Castleford used to buzz on to York with the soldiers. There used to be no end of 'em forget to go to work and get on with the soldiers … Oh they were fast, yeah, they never turned up.

Elsie Slater

Women's Patrols' were established to monitor young women seen in the company of soldiers, and Temperance Societies produced petitions to call for the ban of sales of alcohol to women under twenty-one until three months after the end of the war. Others recognised that there was a need to cope with the pressures of life in wartime Britain.

We were making something that was going to kill or maim others. We had relations out there and we were glad to make the munitions, but we also had to think about the ones that were going to be on the end of it, you see. They were youngsters just coming up in life like I was, sixteen or seventeen. They had parents too. That made me feel sad sometimes.

Florence Nield

Rising costs, food shortages and claims that people were profiteering from the war added to the atmosphere of industrial unrest that had marked the years before the war and strikes became increasingly common.

People were starting to turn against the government and against the war. In my family, it was heartbreaking. My father had been killed. My mum had died just after I was born and I was brought up by my grandmother, my father's mother. She was devastated by my father's death. Her hair turned white in a couple of weeks. I remember watching her and my grandfather weeping, trying to console each other. And some of my uncles never came back from the war, either. That was what was happening to lots of families in Sheffield. They were exhausted and they were angry. I can only describe it as a dark cloud hanging over us. But Sheffield was a proud city that had fought for its rights, going back to the days of the French Revolution, and that's what it did again in the war. Many times the engineering factories were out on strike.

Bill Moore, Sheffield

There was a growing mood of confrontation between police and pickets in the city:

One day I advised them all to bring a big, thick stick with them because some of the Cossacks [mounted police] had rushed us in Earl Marshall Road. I went to report these Cossacks to the Chief Constable, Major Hall-Dallwood. He said, 'Well, you tell me, Mr Sweeting, how it is that your men went out armed yesterday?' 'Is it really necessary to tell you?' I asked. 'Yes.' 'Well, don't you know that the best line of defence is to be prepared to attack?' They never attacked us again after that.

Albert Sweeting, Sheffield

Some unions, though, were fast gaining a reputation for protecting their members at the expense of other workers and the Amalgamated Society of Engineers were widely mocked during one Sheffield strike. 'A Prayer to Lloyd George' expressed the feelings of other local workers:

> Don't send me in the army George,
> I'm in the ASE.
> Take all the bloody labourers,
> But for God's sake don't take me.
> You want me for a soldier?
> Well that can never be –
> A man of my ability
> And in the ASE!

Scout troops were employed during the summer to bring in the flax harvest. Flax was widely used in building aircraft.

After three years of war and the loss of so many lives, the people were tired. The war had not only spread to every corner of the globe, but had affected every person in the country. Even children had been mobilised. Sewing classes in schools set girls to work sewing sandbags or knitting socks for soldiers at the front. Campaigns were launched to encourage children to collect sphagnum moss from the moors for use in field dressings or conkers that could be processed to produce acetone for use in the munitions factories.

Children volunteered to help in war hospitals and raised money on Flag Days, others found business opportunities flourishing around the army camps:

I was quite popular with the soldiers and started to sell them Sunday papers, also the workmen who lived in the huts on the point, making myself some money in the process … I did not like the fact that when I got friendly with the soldiers they would go to France and I never heard from them again.

Ernie Norwood, eight years old, Holderness

Boy Scouts had been called upon from the start of the war to help guard reservoirs, railway tunnels and other 'vulnerable points' but by 1916, had a vital role to play during air raids:

In case the telephone wires were brought down we were delegated in pairs and we had a beat and when the sirens went we used to go on this beat which was kind of relay, you see. Now my beat was from Bawtry Road ... to Tinsley Terminus and there we were met by two other scouts that had a beat from there to a relay until it went to the police station ... that was a right job, getting out of bed at one o'clock in the morning, go walking up and down there ... we did that as part of a badge that was awarded – the War Service Badge.

H. Middleton, Sheffield Boy Scout

In April 1917 when all available troops were required for foreign service, the Pitsmoor Troop were requested by the military authorities to supply a number of scouts to work with a reduced army team in the Parkwood anti-aircraft gun site. Nine boys signed on, seven for work on the gun and two for the searchlight. These scouts attended thee drills per week and soon became proficient in the duties assigned to them and on May 25 the volunteer detachment was ordered to Spurn Head along with the regular team for a shooting trial. The scout team fired very successfully the rounds allocated to them and were specially commended by the inspecting officer.

'Sheffield Yearbook and Record', 1917

Also out during Zeppelin alerts were post office workers, whose job, even on a normal day, could be harrowing:

We used to go to the houses with mostly distress telegrams, you know, people whose lads had got killed or injured or something like that and it was a bit distressing then ... the neighbours and that would stand in groups and as soon as they saw you of course your uniform was enough to set them off ... they'd say 'oh a telegram girl' and then hang around to see what it was like and then more often than not the person you'd taken it to would be too nervous to open it and she would ask you to open it for her. If it was that someone had got wounded they'd burst out crying and you came away and left them with the neighbours. Sometimes it would be to say they were coming home, that a boy was coming home and then of course they got all excited and you still went about your business.

Margaret Furniss, fifteen-year-old Telegram Girl, in 1917

For families torn apart by the war, the post office provided a vital link. Letters and parcels reached soldiers at the front within a day or two – often faster than they reached parts of the UK Soldiers read and re-read letters from home and families at home treasured penciled letters and field postcards sent from the trenches. Walter Parsonage was born in Wakefield in 1882, left school at the age of twelve and by 1909 had risen to the post of manager of the Kinsley Co-operative Society and married Florence Hampshire. In due course, three children arrived: Jack, Nancy and Molly, who was usually referred to as 'Tiny'. In April 1917, at the age of thirty-five, Walter had to leave his family behind when he received his call up papers to report to Fulford Barracks in York.

My mother said he'd volunteered. That's what she told us when we grew up, and she said [that] Lord Kitchener said that if some more men didn't volunteer the Germans – this is just how she told us as children – would come over and they would actually take over our homes and kill [us].

Nancy Oxby née Parsonage

A few weeks later, Walter wrote from his training camp near Whitley Bay:

Walter Parsonage.

I keep making enquiries for a suitable place for you to have a holiday here, of course you know the drawback of three children, but if you do come we must have them they would receive so much benefit from change of air, & they could see ships & airoplanes & gunboats, submarines & hospital ships & trawlers & sweepers & I could fill a page of what they could see ... tell them all to be good and we shall soon be all at Whitley & paddling & filling buckets with sand & going on a boat in the sea. The airoplanes here can go down a line as low as express trains whip round engine & back again they fly just over the house tops very daring men.

Eventually a place was found and the family visited him for a short holiday, before training ended, and Walter was sent to France. He wrote home regularly and in September, his thoughts were of getting leave:

Like you love I shall be glad to come home & I will be content to sleep in [the] back-yard. I was dreaming I was courting again last night, its always you love. Can we really court again when I come home, with all those imps of kids round us, we'll try & risk it ... (6 September)

I trust everything is alright with you love, & try to carry on for my sake, I know its hard for you darling but its not my wish to stay away ... but here again I can't help it, I'd walk it from here if possible to see any one of the four of you. Cheer up old love, we'll have another honeymoon when I come home & after all I'm trying to do my bit, & there ought to be a living found for those who have had to come out here. Jack will be proud to see his Dad when he returns full marching order, rifle, bayonette, trench tool, mess tins, mug pack and all complete. (12 September)

I have some good pals here & we all chip together share anything we have & it's the best way. With the rough element I am stronger than I used to be & soon put a fist up, which soon settles any bother. I always think this if I get a nice Blighty it doesn't matter how I get it ... I feel that all is for the best, & we shall meet again. I shall be strengthened & love you all the more. My mind will be broadened & I shall think more of home & my dear children ... We are all fed up with the war, but we want to drive the Huns back to their own country & come out on top. They are bastards, forgive the word & they do some awful things to those they capture. Some stock of Hun prisoners have passed through our hands lately to go lower down to base. If they only knew it they have a bon time, everything of the best & little work to do. We have had salmon & cake marmalade, jam, marge, stew, bacon, porridge, Rice pudding, Raisons, dates, cheese, matches), cigs, & tobacco, candles, oil, biscuits, & 4 lengths 2 flanette this week to clean rifles, surely we are winning. (21 September)

Fancy Jack wondering what I was having to tea. I often try to picture you round the tea table, with the white cloth on. We always use the floor for our table & sit on the same. We do fairly well, but give me a decent meal at home. One meal at home is worth three in army. You know how I used to like a bit of supper, but in army there is no supper. We all hope the war will soon be over, & then we'll have a do. (29 September)

His wife Florrie tried to keep him up to date with news from home:

I do hope you will always be lucky love and come home some day, I often wonder if you look any different. Do you know Bob Darbyshire has gone under, his wife got official news yesterday & it was reported you love were badly wounded so you can guess how relieved I was to get your [Post Card] I wonder who sets tales about. I heard Ned Womersley is wounded I think from what I hear he was in the same camp as Bob Darbyshire when a shell dropped on them. Henry, White died last Sunday at a nursing home in Leeds. (24 October)

Like many men, Walter had heard the rumours about rising food and rent costs:

I am fairly well & want for nothing, you must not send any money love, as things are too dear in England. I get 5 *Franks* a week & this is plenty for me, as my wants are simple, & we have an issue of tobacco ... I must really try to send you a bit, if things are so dear. I wish you had been anywhere near me, as we have had lots of spare rations dumped on us, worst of it is, we have always to dump them, as we cannot carry much besides our packs, 2 gas helmets, rifle, 120 rounds, haversacks, equipment etc etc, about 100lbs including iron rations, 2 days rations & water. (2 November)

December approached with no sign of leave – usually granted after one year of service – and Florrie prepared for their first Christmas apart:

I hope that your luck will continue, & that you will soon come home to us. You don't know how much I am looking forward to you coming home, only it does seem a long time off. I dreamt the other night you had come home for Christmas for seven days & wasn't I just disappointed when I woke up. Jack Nan & Tiny ... are quite delighted to think you will be having a good feed at Xmas. We are stopping here, I would rather, do you know if I go away I feel as though I were missing your letters or something. I often wonder if you will knock me up some night, but no such luck yet. (19 December)

I do hope you will be behind lines for a week or two. Soon be Xmas now. I had a nice surprise from club £1 to draw, it has come in useful for us for extras for Christmas, I shall give the kiddies a good time love, I have been able to get a bit extra butter, marg & tea at shop this week, Mary sent us a plumb pudding & lots of other things, which is just like her good nature. Lizzie has sent Jack a flashlight & book, & other things for stockings. Mrs Wainwright has given us a young cockerel, one of the black ones its only small but will be nice and tender So don't you think we shall have a good time, the kiddies will, they don't understand what war is yet. They only know Daddy is a long time away. Oh that you could come home love. We would have a real Christmas. Never mind dear we will have a good time when you do come home, & hope you wont be long. I had another of your letters returned on Sat, one I sent to you on 19 Nov, the first after you had been wounded, I wonder why you don't get them. That is the 3 I've had returned, I'm always writing to you love, I hope you will get them when you get back to Battalion again. I sent you a parcel last week & two letters. Red Cross Society have I think sent you 5s & your Mother has sent a parcel so I hope you will get them all … its awful to think of you being wet through & my heart aches to think about it all, Oh that the war would end. G. Clarke got married a week last Sat, never mentioned it at all, I haven't seen Mrs Turner since, I expect she will be alright now. Jim Hoyle is expecting coming home anytime now, his year is up. Mr Porter joined up & joined Army Ordinance Corps, so don't suppose he will have to rough it like you. Yes Jack got his knife alright & is delighted with it. We are all quite well & are looking forward to Daddy coming home, you have been in France nearly six months, hope you are as lucky the next six but what a long time to look forward to, we shall not want you to go back again, I didn't get my rent etc as I told you I had applied for. Worse luck. But thought I would try. It has been cold here this last week. Some snow & frost but a thaw has now set in. So we shall have plenty of dirt for Xmas.

Will finish now dear & wishing you the best of luck in the New Year & hope you have a fairly good time, remember me to your pals those I know, I guess you are all fed up & would like to be home again, I think you ought to have leave every 3 months a year is such a long time to wait we are always thinking of you dear, & if I could I would change places with you for a time but I can do nothing only keep children well and wait for your return.

God bless you and keep you safe

All my love, Yrs lovingly

X Florrie XXX

J, N. & M. XXXXX

I have been making paper flowers for kiddies & Nancy has bought some mistletoe, they keep kissing each other under it. (23 December)

My dearest Florrie,

I received 5 letters & your parcel on 24th for which I thank you very much. I also got 4 letters & parcels from Lizzie & 5s Postal Order from Mrs Elliott. We happened to be out of line on reserve for Xmas so that with the help of parcels & our own Battalion dinner I had a good time. Plenty of pork, ham, beer, rum etc etc. Concert at night. I shared cake out to my pals who had been unlucky & got nothing reserving a big piece for myself. You have sent a good selection & I enjoyed the content very much. I was thinking & wondering of you love all Christmas day. I would have enjoyed myself much better with you love if only I had dry bread to eat. I wonder what sort of a time you and my J. N. M. have had love. Lizzie has sent word that she had a present ready for each, did these come. I sent you our Battalion Christmas Card, all I had chance to do.

Tonight my sergeant goes on leave to Sheffield & I have given him 5 Franks to send a little parcel of sweets etc to J. N. M. for Xmas or New Year. We cannot send from here as we are not in civil parts. I am fairly well, there is some talk of peace, but it sounds more like pieces here, the guns play hell all day & night. I have had that lobster for tea, & am just boiling & now eaten my Xmas pudding & it's a treat. We have a good fire in brasier on hut floor. Its rather a bad light to write by but I know you wont bother about the writing. It's a treat to be warm a bit. We have had a lot of frost & snow I saw some ice today 14 inches thick. Its cold at night, we have 2 blankets each while we are out. In line no blankets too heavy to carry. I would have given anything to have spent Xmas with you love, & I have felt it more than anything else out here to think of you my darling, lonely at home & my dear children it put the wind up me.

So Geo Clarke has married Mrs Turner after all. I only hope she is good to the children. Poor Mrs Clarke I often think of her coming to our house & having a chat. I don't think I could ever fancy another love, I'm too much in love with you yet dear. I shall always love you dear it's no duty, no burden it's just I can't help it. If I am spared to return to you I will see that I will make the rest of your life happy. I hope you have a happy new year & the old war soon over. My chums said the cake was fine & Cheshire Cheese is a change all Canadian [cheese] in Army. I have put my new socks on & my feet feel better. Parcels are expensive so don't send another in hurry I'm alright. Hope you get £1 from Club, to get the kids something. God bless you all every hour of the day.

Yours lovingly

Walter XXXXX

JNM XXXXX

Parcel of [sweets] coming. (26 December)

True to his word, Walter's sergeant sent a package of sweets to the children along with a note for Florrie:

Dear Madam do not worrie about your husband he looks in the best of Health & i hope he gets back home again to you all safe & sound. he is at present near Ypres [he] Is going on fine hoping that he keep well till it is all over Well I wish you all a Happy New Year.
I remain your obedient servant
Sgt Langton

On 18 January a telegram arrived from No 2 Infantry Records office, York. Walter's sister tried to find out what had happened:

Jan 28/18
Dear Miss Parsonage,
Your letter of the 24th has been handed to me. I was not with the platoon containing your brother at the time he met his death but I am able to give you some particulars of the unfortunate occurrence. With a party of other men [he] was parading to do some work in the front line. A shell burst quite close to the party & a fragment of it struck him piercing his steel helmet & severely wounding him in the head. He was rendered unconscious at once & passed away shortly after arrival at the dressing station. He would have suffered no pain. He was properly buried in a cemetery & his grave will be cared for & is marked by a cross. I will find out if possible the number of the cemetery then you can write to the officer in charge & possibly get a photo of your brother's grave. I sympathise very much with you in your sorrow. Although death stalks among us day & night we feel the loss of every single officer & man & realize that to some home each death brings sorrow and suffering. Let me ask you not to grieve. You have this consolation that he gave his life for his country & died a soldier & a man. The manner of his death proves his worth & entitles him to a place with the great heroes who have given up their all for the cause of freedom & right. Death comes to us all sooner or later & how could one die better than giving up his life for other & then may not the awakening in the other sphere be happy & glorious. Time will heal the sharpness of your sorrow & then you will live looking forward to the time when you will meet your brother again in another land where wars & death shall never come & you will be proud he was faithful until death.
Yours Sincerely
Cecil James 2/Lt
A Coy 1/5 K...
B...France

Dear Mrs Parsonage, I have the Deepest sympathy in which to let you know that it is true that your husband died of wounds, they told me when I got back that

I had lost one of my best men, so you can guess how sorry I am to lose him & I hope you will accept my deepest sympathy. The boys told me that your husband was hit with a piece off a shell and died soon after without saying anything at all. I know what a shock it would be to you after me telling you how well he looked, which he did & a finer soldier you could not wish to see or meet and he was liked by all the boys. If I can do anything for you I shall only be too pleased, so do not be afraid to write and let me know, I shall have to close now hoping that you are able to stand the strain and that your children soon grow up to look after you hoping that I have the luck to get through this terrible war then I will come and see you & the children. Hoping that they & you are in the best of health & keep so.

I remain your obedient servant

Sgt A. Langton

Florrie was left to explain to the children that their beloved Daddy would not be coming home.

6

1918:
'THEY SHALL GROW NOT OLD...'

By 1918, American troops were beginning to appear on the Western Front and the tide began to turn. The revolution of late 1917 had effectively forced Russia out of the war, freeing up many thousands of German troops to reinforce the Western Front. In a desperate attempt to break the allied lines before the build-up of US forces could be completed, at 4.40 a.m. on 21 March, 6,000 German guns, supported by 3,000 trench mortars, rained 1, 60,000 shells onto the British trenches as specially trained 'Stormtroopers' crept through thick fog and smoke to infiltrate the lines and pave the way for an attack by sixty-six divisions of infantry.

In the middle of the night, we runners were turned out as urgent messages had to be delivered to recall outlying detachments. Jerry had broken through our lines and was rapidly sweeping all before him. I was detailed to contact our boxing team and lead them to a point where the whole battalion was to be picked up by buses and rushed to the line. We got into 'battle order', piled our packs in a field (we never saw them again, or our personal effects) and followed our guide across country to a line of old trenches which were held by the remnants of a battalion who had been badly cut up and had been retiring for days. We took over from them, stayed that night in those trenches, then, in daylight, began to retire.

Private Arthur Pearson, Leeds Pals

The Kaiserschlacht (Emperor's Battle) of 1918 almost broke through the British lines.

We arrived, after a twelve hour ride, at a lonely spot on the shell scarred road, from which we could see several villages on fire, the ruddy glow lighting the blackness for miles. Here, after dumping all unnecessaries, we were collected together … and then we were quietly told that our task was to hold a trench one foot deep and to hold it at all costs.

Private Percy Barlow, Leeds Pals

About 9 a.m. (April 9th) wounded soldiers were being hurried through the streets, and Fritz was shelling heavily. He put about 6,000 gas and other shells into the village – every yard was marked. Our office was blown to atoms. It was awful to see. Nothing but a flattened place in six hours – dead horses and soldiers all over. I got the order to pack my kit (if possible) and, clear out the best way I could. The worst of it was Fritz was covering two miles past the village and it was not safe until we got two miles away. I was packing my kit when the bottom room of the billet was blown in, and the staircase gave way. I was very lucky not to get hit. Many wounded were lying all about. A team of horses, taking ammunition up to the guns, was blown up twenty yards in front of me. I had to rest in a passage to get my wind, and I gave some water to an artillery driver who was badly wounded. I then laid down in a trench with some infantry and later got away a few miles. Here the Company came up in twos and threes; some are wounded, and some missing. At tea time, Fritz started shelling us as he advanced, and when he advances he shells the road for miles. This occurred for two more days as he advanced. Only six of our men got their kits; Fritz got the rest. He was putting his machine-guns on the village just as I left. I have slept on the roads for two nights, just as I was, like a top.

Private Percy W. Taylor, of Adelaide Street, Todmorden

The whole 'show' has been absolute Hell. Several times we have been surrounded, and yet have managed to get away. There have been times when we have been almost touching the Boche – he with vastly superior numbers – and it has been a case of giving ourselves up or running for it, and we have run for it, and some of us live to fight another day. I felt an awful coward the first time I ran, but the only alternative was to become a prisoner. Once I was shot at by a party of Boches at under fifty yards range … The nights have been very cold, and sleep an unheard of thing, just an odd hour here and there … I cannot as I said before tell you all, what I have written only gives a tiny fraction of what has happened, I thank God I am alive to tell it.

Lieutenant Cecil Slack, 4th East Yorkshires

There is no other course open to us but to fight it out, every position must be held to the last man. There must be no retirement; with our backs to the wall and believing in the justice of our cause each of us must fight on to the end. The safety of our homes and the freedom of mankind alike depend upon the conduct of each one of us at this critical moment.

General Haig, 11 April 1918

Fortunately for the British, the German army was suffering the impact of years of blockade by the Royal Navy and the attackers lost momentum as troops looted British supply dumps for food and equipment but by the time the danger passed, many thousands of men had been taken prisoner. Stories of atrocities in Belgium in 1914 were still widely believed:

I hated them. There you are. I'm not going to say that I didn't. And as now, I don't like them. When you come to realise all the things that they did to people; to human beings. Everyone heard about what they were doing, the Germans, to people. If they found a man that was injured, they didn't used to try and get him put right. They used to shoot him, to put him out of his misery, they used to say. They hardly ever took any prisoners the Germans, oh no.

Henry Dotchin, Middlesbrough

Such stories affected the way British soldiers treated German prisoners:

Nearly every instructor in the mess could quote specific instances of prisoners having been murdered on the way back ... the [prisoner escorts] would report on arrival at headquarters that a German shell had killed the prisoners and no questions would be asked ... At all events, most overseas men, and some British troops, made atrocities against prisoners a boast, not a confession.

Robert Graves, *Goodbye to All That*

Usually, though, the treatment of prisoners by both sides was rough but fair:

It was round about four o'clock in the afternoon. I was lookout but it was foggy, you couldn't see your hand in front of your face. We were in a dugout and there was a lot of noise. We went to have a look and we could hear talking at the other end of this trench, but we didn't know they were Germans, we thought they were our lads. I says to Tommy Wetton, 'There's something doing down there, Tommy. I'll have a walk out and see what's going off'. He said he couldn't understand it. I'd been out two or three minutes when I looked over the top of this trench and I saw this German, then 'whoosh' a grenade went up. He'd thrown a 'tatie-masher' at me. Some of the shrapnel hit him first then it hit me on the hand and on the leg as well. I set off to walk but my leg gave way and I fell over. I must say this, the Germans were very good to me. They picked me up and put me on a stretcher and took me to their first aid post. All the wounded Germans were lying there. I was interrogated three times at three different places. At the third interrogation there were four guards, two at the front and two at the back. They took me to a Colonel with a Belgian interpreter. It was difficult. The Colonel asked me if I wanted a cigarette. He got this cigarette lighter out and it was the first time I'd seen one like that. It was like a revolver. I thought he was going to fire a shot at me. We both laughed. That interrogation went on for over an hour. I told them a pack of lies. I told 'em I knew nothing at all about soldiers but they'd got a first class shot and they didn't know. The night we'd moved up I'd been given another stripe and a needle and cotton to sew it on with. I'd a badge for being a first class shot as well. As we were going up I ripped the lot off, chucked 'em in a trench and threw a stone on them. By God, it's a good job I did because if they'd got that first class badge, they were offering money for a first class Lewis gunner. I don't know what told me to do it, but I was captured soon after. I spent the rest of the war in prisoner of war camps at Minden, Munster and Essen, and then a camp at Oberhausen.

Private Ossie Burgess, 14th York and Lancaster Regiment

The priority for many was the collection of 'souvenirs' from their prisoners, as a 1918 song from the German Prisoner of War Camp at Skipton noted:

> War einst ein deutsche Offizier,
> Halt! Who comes there?
> Und is jetzt taken prisoner,
> All correct, Sir!
> The watsch and money
> All Souvenir
> For focking Tommy

We never went into a camp, we were just behind the lines all the time. When Jerry advanced we went with them; when he retreated after our 1918 'Big Push' we went back with them. All the guards were old men, the young men were up in the line. I did see a lot of Germans when I was taken prisoner, a lot of dead ones. There were a lot of English and Portuguese lying around too. 'Port and Beans' we used to call them. For the first week that's all we were doing, collecting the dead in a handcart. The place where we buried them was on a hillside and we put twenty in a grave about three feet deep. We'd put a wooden cross above them with the inscription '20 British soldiers'. The Germans took their boots off them. They took them off us. I had to wear a pair of Dutch clogs. The food was terrible. We used to have a quarter of a loaf of black bread and German sausage. We'd have a bowl of sauerkraut. It was just water with cabbage and two pieces of horsemeat floating on the top. By that time the Germans had very little food for themselves. I was about eight stone when I landed back home and used to weigh twelve.

Private George Armitage Nichols, Barnsley Pals

Kapitan Sachsse was captured in 1917 and taken to a camp near Ripon before being sent to a Kriegsgefangenenlager (Prisoner of War) camp at Skipton:

The days of the move came. On the 17, 19 and 21 January, fifty prisoners paraded in the grey dawn. [The weather was freezing and] according to credible witnesses, on 9 January even one of the English guards was found frozen – they were mostly old people. Dragged from their sweet sleep and away from drinking their coffee, the prisoners were delivered into the hands of interpreters and 'sergeants' and stripped ready to be searched. Inventive prisoners found ways of smuggling through such valuables as money, compasses and other objects but the modest historian cannot describe the parts of the body used to hide the treasures.

Soon came the order to 'open double gate' and we were then homeless on the snow- and ice-covered road. With a tender look at the pitiful possessions in our hands, I was reminded of the old saying *Omnia mea mecum porto* ['All that's mine I carry with me.']. Prodded into rows of four by watchful British bayonets, we set out and marched on the smooth road uphill and downhill through the mountains, passing the clean village houses and small farms with castle-like gates and stone fences across the barren winter land. Sheep and cattle, their existence being dull, stood and stared as we passed by. After two hours of strenuous marching we got down to Masham, the railway terminus, where we were loaded along with our guards into a comfortable car and soon, the train set out into the rolling Yorkshire countryside.

In a toasty warm, red soft plush carriage we tried to chat in broken English with our Tommy guards. They were old people, without any real hatred of 'Fritz'; they were honest and made no secret of their dislike of the endless war. Weeton, Harthington, Harrogate and Ripon rushed past us. At each stop, curiously, but peacefully, Albion's sons admired the 'Huns'. One or two ladies were snippy and made a stand against the 'Huns' but they were not very attractive women, better from the back view and not the classic beauty of the lovely German Gretchen look we missed so much.

Finally, the train arrived in Leeds where smoke from thousands of chimneys guided us and where we felt England's panting breath against the pressure of Germany's iron fist. We left our car here, and admired the giant signs alongside the station urging people to 'Buy War Bonds'. We then climbed aboard a new train. The old guard left us, and a security team from Skipton took over to accompany their valuable cargo the rest of the way. The English officer leading them behaved very graciously: a great man of an enviably plump body and round, sensual face. His stately chin was receding and seemed to join straight into his neck and several times he seemed to thrust it forward in a jutting movement creating the comfortable, powerful image of exquisitely trained triple chins. In memory of our gas masks in the field, from then on we always referred to him as 'Three layers'. He brought us comforting news: the new Camp Commander is a gentle, mild man and the conditions were good. As we travelled on, we became more tense. The train took us in a graceful valley, where a river (the

Aire) threaded its way alongside the railway. After passing Keighley, we reached our goal at last at about three o'clock in the afternoon: Skipton.

And there stood our new dignified and joyful camp Adjutant! How few of us even know his real name! His first words, 'I can kill you' set the tone for our stay at Skipton. A small, slightly built man with short legs, searching eyes and a nose discoloured by drink, a quiet suspicion developed within us that he was mostly bluster and the name 'Icankillyou' immediately stuck. A short, sharp tap to his cap to acknowledge our guards and we were handed over to his care. It seemed he wanted to show that he alone made up for the less disciplined officers under his command.

We wondered about the three black ribbons fluttering behind his cap [he was from a highland regiment and wore a Glengarry] as he formed us up on the station forecourt and ordered her into a column of march. In tight step we walked through Skipton's streets. The whole town was standing in dignified silence along the sidewalks to watch as we moved down the road in a dark mass. Their staid faces showed surprise and curiosity as here and there a finger pointed out particular prisoners and an occasional joke was made. On all their faces was an obvious pleasure to see Huns, captured in battle and now in English hands! And since we German officers stepped through I felt a mixture of feelings. I noted in my diary;

'A feeling of defencelessness came over me among these thousands of British eyes. What was in me, my sense of being a warrior seemed torn before those eyes and profaned. I had to cast my eyes down with shame. A sense of nothing in my poor life having prepared me for this. I was ashamed for my country. Like me, my sneering superior Geüber seemed no longer to be himself.'

Little 'Icankillyou' was rumoured to have been Commander of a camp for German prisoners in France and to have threatened reluctant Germans with a great British gun and his awful, familiar power crazy cry of 'I can kill you'. Another report said he had even carried out the threat, murdering an unarmed German officer in a raging fury, still shouting 'I can kill you'. Perhaps one day we'll find the truth.

Conditions at Skipton were good. Men were put to work on nearby farms and officers, who could not be ordered to work under the terms of the Geneva Convention, were allowed escorted visits into Skipton to pass the time. British prisoners in Germany were also put to work while their officers, having signed a formal 'parole' document, were on their honour not to try to escape when allowed out of the camp. Both sides respected the promise – after all, any breach would mean and end to the practice. When in camp, though, thoughts turned to how to get home:

Die Häupter unserer Lieban :

Herr Major. Kill vou".

Major 'Icankillyou'.

The first English camp I was taken to as a German prisoner of war in July 1917 was Colsterdale, near Masham, up north in Yorkshire, and I hope it will be taken in good part when I say that I didn't want to stay there. I tried several times to get through the barbed wire and I also took part in one of the tunnelling schemes which was, however, discovered by the British just before the tunnel was completed. Then one fine day I hit upon the idea of just walking out through the gate disguised as our English canteen manager, who was about my size and figure – his name was Mr Budd ... So evening after evening I started observing closely his every movement on leaving the camp, and noticed to my satisfaction that the sentries never asked him for the password. Everybody knew Mr Budd too well for that. This was also, of course, rather a drawback; but my idea was to do the thing in the evening after dark. I'd been informed – I think quite wrongly – that every male passenger in those war days was supposed to produce a pass or other document when booking a railway ticket, particularly when travelling to London, and as I didn't feel like walking the whole way there I decided to travel as a woman.

We had private codes between the camps and our people at home so I sent a message to my mother asking her to send me every conceivable thing which I should need for this disguise. After some time I received news that a wig was arriving camouflaged as tobacco; that all sorts of fake jewellery, a compass and similar handy things had been sent off in marmalade jars, or baked in a cake – and, last but not least, that I would soon receive a large quilt with a skirt, petticoat, veil, some sort of a hat, silk stockings and a nice silk coat all sewn up in it. I had asked for everything in black, even the necklace and brooches, as I wanted to look like a poor widow so that people on the trains wouldn't speak to me as freely as if I were dressed as a giddy young girl.

Then I heard rumours of Mr Budd being transferred to some other camp, so I couldn't afford to wait for the arrival of these mysterious packages and began collecting an outfit in the camp. My skirt was made out of an old blanket and the hat and muff were mostly composed of parts of fur waistcoats. We had plenty of fancy costumes in the camp, beautiful wigs, hats, and so on, but they were all under 'word of honour not to be used except for theatrical purposes, and so of course I couldn't use them.

Then the great day arrived and I put on all the clothes, man and woman's mixed together so that I was able to change from one to the other with a few slight manipulations. I approached the gate disguised as Mr Budd with a false moustache and a pair of spectacles, worn exactly the way Mr Budd wore them. My cap, mackintosh and bag were also exact replicas of the ones with which Mr Budd used to leave the camp every evening. Even the most pessimistic of my friends thought I really was Mr Budd when they saw me. Mr Budd was in the habit of leaving camp about 8 p.m. and I had timed my attempt for about ten minutes to eight. Meanwhile a few friends of mine would keep the real Mr Budd busy in the canteen and as the sentries were usually changed at 8 o'clock sharp I was sure that the new sentry would not be surprised to see the real Mr Budd leaving camp. So off I went straight to the gate gaily smoking my pipe as if after a good day at the canteen. A few yards from it I shouted 'Guard' as this was the way Mr Budd used to announce himself day by day. The sentry called out, 'Who's there?' 'Budd,' I answered. 'Right', he said and opened the big door.

I walked slowly down the street from the camp towards Masham station. I had about a two-hours walk before me; but I hadn't gone more than fifty yards when I espied our Commandant coming towards me. Within a fraction of a second I had torn off the moustache and spectacles as, of course, I didn't want the Colonel to address the false Mr Budd. As I passed him I just said 'Good evening' and so did he. A little further on I decided to change into a woman. This was only a matter of a few seconds. I exchanged Mr Budd's cap with the woman's hat and veil which I carried in my bag and took off my mackintosh, which covered a navy-blue civilian jacket, trimmed with all sorts of lace and bows. My skirt was hitched up with a leather belt round my hips so I had only to undo the belt to release the skirt. Luckily for me skirts in those days reached down to the ground, so my leggings were completely covered by the skirt and couldn't be seen in the dark. I met some Tommies on the road, and they all behaved very decently; they all bade me 'good evening', and none of them insisted on starting a conversation with the very reserved woman who did not even reply to their 'good evening'. Only once I was a bit troubled, by a shepherd's dog, but he soon withdrew when the strange woman took something out of her muff and sprinkled it on the road. It is very important for an escaper always to carry a box of pepper to defend himself against dogs.

I'd been walking now for quite some time, making good progress towards the station of Masham, when I noticed three soldiers following me and overtaking me. One of them was equipped with a rifle with fixed bayonet and I knew that this must surely be a sentry from the camp as there were no other military in the neighbourhood. I at once thought of throwing away my bag which might so easily give me away, but anything of that sort would immediately have aroused suspicion. The soldiers came steadily closer and closer until they finally overtook me. They then stopped and said 'Good evening miss. Have you by any chance seen a man with a bag like yours? A prisoner of war has escaped and we are out looking for him'. Well I tried for a time, really only a very short time, to speak in a high voice, telling them please not to bother a decent young girl by starting a conversation with her, but they all said they might as well have a look at the bag I carried. I refused, of course, but it was only a matter of another few seconds before I realized that it was all over with me.

Heinz Justus

After being returned to camp, Justus was sentenced to a few weeks at Chelmsford prison before a transfer to Holyport. After a few more escape attempts, he was put on a train bound for Lofthouse Park camp near Wakefield. Just outside South Elmsall, he jumped from the train and made his way to Doncaster, calmly going to a performance of *You Are Spotted* at the local theatre to pass the time until the next London bound train was due. Disguised this time by just a mackintosh over his military tunic, he blended in with the London crowds as he searched for a neutral ship that might take him home.

There was a Red Cross Day on or something, and soon I was stopped in the street by a kind elderly lady who insisted on selling me a little Union Jack which she tried to pin on my mackintosh. However the pin wouldn't go through and the trouble was that she always stabbed against the Iron Cross which I was wearing on my tunic.

Heinz Justus

Justus managed to reach Cardiff docks, but fell ill and was eventually forced to hand himself in. After another spell at Chelmsford he returned

Ernest Pearce enlisted in the 14th York and Lancasters at the age of fifteen, and was taken prisoner in the Kaiserschlacht of 1918. He escaped through the camp sewers and made it to neutral Holland.

to spend the rest of his war at Lofthouse Park, Wakefield. Meanwhile, British prisoners were busily tunnelling out of their camps, too. Eighteen-year-old Ernest Pearce of the York and Lancasters had been captured in the March offensive and taken to Dulmen in Westphalia where he, accompanied by a Frenchman and a Highlander named Alex Miller, promptly found a way out via the camp sewers.

We had been living on cabbage leaves, raw potatoes and grass for over a week, and our boots and socks were worn away so that we were walking almost on the dubbing; but we made good progress considering ... In the early morning we came to some beautiful gardens, with sentry boxes posted here and there. It looked quite nice. The sentries let us pass unchallenged ... and further on we came to some arc lights which turned out to be Roermund railhead in [neutral] Holland ... Soldiers rushed out to see us and an officer who spoke English said, 'Your breakfast is ready'.

Ernest Pearce

As the German offensive ground to a halt, the allies began to respond. Slowly, the battle turned. In July, the 62nd West Riding Division took part in a coalition battle alongside French, American and Italian troops to force the Germans back from the Marne, near Paris. In August, British forces won a major victory over the Germans near Cambrai and so began the 'Last Hundred Days' when, at great cost, the British pushed the Germans further and further back until, in November, a German delegation, led by Matthias Erzberger, crossed the line to discuss the end of the war. Germany was facing revolution and people had taken to the streets as a result of chronic food shortages caused by the British naval blockade. After three days of intense negotiations in a rail siding just outside of Compiegne, the German delegation signed the terms of the Armistice at 05.10 a.m. on 11 November. The news reached London half an hour later and celebrations began before most soldiers even knew about the Armistice. In London, Big Ben was rung for the first time since the start of the war in August 1914. In Paris, gas lamps were lit for the first time in four years. But on the Western Front, many tens of thousands of soldiers assumed that it was just another day in the war and officers ordered their men into combat.

At 9.30 a.m. Private George Edwin Ellison, a former coal miner from Leeds, was serving with the 5th Royal Irish Lancers and scouting on the outskirts of the Belgian town of Mons where German soldiers had been reported in a wood. At forty, Ellison had been in the regular Army in 1914 and after four years was now back where his war began. Soon, he would be able to return home to his wife Hannah and their four-year-old son, James, who had never really known his father. And then a shot rang out. George was dead – the last British soldier to be killed in action in the First World War.

Armistice Day, November 11 1918
South of Maubeuge
Troops marching along the roads by platoons at intervals – a fresh autumn day. An early telegram has given the expected news 'operations will cease at 11 a.m. 'The men cannot grasp it – they have become so used to this soldier life, so numbed to endurance that they find it hard to believe they can live otherwise. At 11 o'clock, under orders (and for that reason only!) the troops are halted and give three cheers – but there is no enthusiasm. Of course they are glad it is all over – but they do not realise it. And that was the end of the greatest war that history has ever known.

Major Lancelot Spicer, 9th KOYLI

Sweetheart – well it has come at least. The day we have always longed for, for four weary years. I got it over the 'phone today at 9.50am from Brigade. It's surprising how we all took it. Practically no excitement – I suppose really our feelings are too deep. We are carrying on just as usual. I've been writing my history of the last battle. I suppose really it's a greater relief to you than me. I ought to be, and am, very thankful I've come through.

Major S. G. Beaumont, 24th KOYLI

When the news reached Hull the streets in the city centre were filled with anticipatory crowds ... Gradually the national flags were unfurled from the public buildings, and an hour later the allied ships in the docks were gaily dressed. Thousands of flags were sold in the streets and during the afternoon bluejackets and soldiers were parading through the thoroughfares, dancing, singing patriotic songs and letting off booming fireworks. The demeanour of the general public was significant. There was plainly in every heart a feeling of thankfulness that hostilities had ceased. At Dewsbury the official news was announced from the Town Hall steps about noon by the Mayor ... By that time all the places of business were closed and the town was rapidly decorated with flags and banners. A thanksgiving service was held in front of the Town Hall at which there was an impressive spectacle. It is estimated that well over 12,000 people were present ... Leeds threw off all restraint and gave itself up to whole-hearted, whole-souled enthusiasm. Most of the employers, on hearing the news, at once closed down for the afternoon and where no official move was made in this direction the workforce simply took French leave ... the workers at the shell-filling factory (mostly women) were sent back to Leeds by special train ... By noon the centre of the city was alive with shouting, singing and merry-making crowds.

Barnsley Chronicle

It is quite impossible to describe the feeling of relief. Only those who were there could appreciate it fully.

Second Lieutenant Clifford Carter, 2nd York and Lancaster.

The war was over but now began the grim task of clearing the battlefields.

The Padre asked me if I would accompany him to visit our old front line and No Man's Land, which was littered with British dead. Ours were in lines where they had fallen. They were just skeletons in khaki rags and their equipment. We walked up to the old German wire. The Padre had brought a friend with him and the three of us turned back to look towards our lines. Then the Padre said a prayer for the dead and we sang Hymn number 437 from Hymns Ancient and Modern, 'For All the Saints'. I've still got that hymn book, it holds a very poignant memory for me. Next morning the dead were buried by an overnight fall of snow. It was to be some weeks before No Man's Land was cleared when V Corps began to make new cemeteries to lay our friends to rest.

Lance Corporal J. R. Glenn, Sheffield Pals

After the war had finished, we were walking across the fields, picking up rifles and bombs and anything else to do with the war. Two of our lads came across some shells that had been primed but never fired. They got all these shells and picked them up. They were coming to the dump when one of the shells slipped off his arm and hit the striking pin and exploded. They were both killed. It was terrible – they were just doing a duty of cleaning the countryside for the French folk.

Pte Arthur Barrowclough, Duke of Wellington's Regiment

After the war there were so many widows and mothers, asking if they could come over to France. It all seemed so far away to them, and if they could just come to France, they would feel nearer and more in touch with their sons – and perhaps know a little more than they had been told before. There were one or two men still in hospital, but on the whole it wasn't that that brought the women over.

Mrs B. Brooke, Volunteer Guide and Escort

The war was not yet over: the Armistice was just a ceasefire to allow peace negotiations to begin. Troops needed to be kept ready in case the Germans used the lull to regroup their forces, and so the process of demobilising the army was slow and methodical. Some who had been among the first to enlist, giving up their jobs to do so, now found themselves listed as having no job and therefore among the last to be released.

April 12 1919 was our day of liberation, to the great annoyance of those who were still waiting to see their boys demobbed from the army. 'Why should skunks and shirkers get free before men who have been fighting for their country?'

Bert Brocklesby, Imprisoned Conscientious Objector

One by one, the men came home:

The first day home, at dinner time, there was just my mother, father and me at home, but there were seven places laid at the table. I asked why, when there were only three of us. My mother said, 'We have some German prisoners working in the brick works and I try to make them a bit of dinner, because I thought the Germans would be looking after you.' I said, 'Mother, they gave us nothing. I went down to seven stone'. 'Yes – but you are back

Street party, Bradford.

home and they're still here.' She was that sort of woman. 'I thought I would make them a bit of dinner – and I thought you could take it out to them. I said, 'All right, mother – put a bit of arsenic on it and I will take it out.' She said, 'Don't be like that – at least you are back home'. So I said I'd take the food out to the German prisoners – a plateful of the same food as we were having. I told her about the conditions in Germany but she wouldn't believe me. There was one Bavarian chap there – he was nice and he wanted to have a talk about what they had done to us. It was just a day later that my brother got home – and my mother was so relieved. She kept saying, 'He's not coming back. I know it. I know it. You might as well tell me the truth'. I said, 'No you WILL finally see him tomorrow'. And she did.

We got a fortnight's leave, and I began to eat normally again – but I had to be careful. We had been warned that after being starved for so long, we could do ourselves more harm than good. The day after my leave ended, I had to report to York, and the day after that I went up to Whitley Bay to a convalescent home. We were treated very well there, and we didn't do any parades or work. We were there as invalids, to get ourselves better again.

I couldn't wait to be demobilised. I wanted to get out as quickly as I could. I'd had more than enough of the Army. I'd joined up for the duration and the duration had come and gone. Now I wanted to be back in civilian life. We got forms to fill and I realized that it depended very much on what sort of work you did, how and when you were demobilised. There were certain areas of industry where they wanted to get you back at work. Unfortunately mine wasn't very important. My father ran brickworks, and I knew bricks would be required because there was a lot of building and repair work to be done. I said to my father, 'If I put myself down as a brick and tile worker, can you find me a job for a week or two?' He said he could, so I put that on the form and I got an early discharge.

The only thing I do resent is to do with my health. I went in as A1, and I came out B2. At the only examination I got after the war, they checked my heart and took my pulse – saw I was still breathing and said I was A1 – but I should have been classed as B2. I ought to have pressed them about that, because I had been gassed and slightly wounded and been reduced to a terrible state. I ought to have pressed for another examination, but I just wanted to be out. One friend of mine got a wound in his eye the first day in action. He got a full pension for the rest of his life. That is what I objected to! One day in the trenches, he got a small wound and was awarded a full pension. I got nothing.

If you had a job before the war and you volunteered to join up, they had to give you your job back after the war. When I went back to my old job, the boss had got a couple of girls in. We had a chat and the manager said that the girls would have to leave because I wanted my job back, but he said that he would rather keep them on. I said we'd see about that, but then one day my mother told me that a man who owned two shops in the village – a grocers and a chemist – would like to see me. He asked me if I'd like to work for him, and I said I'd love to. He said he'd pay me £2-10 shillings a week – and I didn't know what money was worth, but it was more than I had been getting when I joined up.

Private Walter Hare, 15th West Yorkshires

I was in the cloth export section with a firm called Sharp, Sonnenthal & Company. I was only nineteen, and just a bit of a superior clerk at the time but I wasn't anything special. When I came back I'd my job to come back to and I will say this about the firm, they were very good. Of course I volunteered, and they paid us half wages all through the war to those of us who joined up voluntary, not those who were called up. At the time I was getting a pound a week, so my mother collected ten shillings all through the war for me. This was a lot of money when I came out, and it seemed very nice to have a hundred pounds to come back to.

Private Fred Rawnsley, Bradford Pals

I believe it was the quickest demobilisation there'd ever been. On 23 December we were still at Dunkirk and then we came across the Channel in the evening and landed at Folkestone. At 10 pm we caught a train through London and we were in Ripon by half past four in the morning. In the afternoon of 24 December we were back at Ripon station where we caught a train to Leeds … We had to make our own way from Leeds. We caught the last train from Leeds to Barnsley between 10 and 11 p.m. There were no buses when we got to Barnsley so we walked to the end of Doncaster Road to catch a bus from there, but they were all full up. We walked a bit further and who should come round but Lewis Burrows in a van. It was like a mini-bus that used to run on market days and being Christmas Eve it was like a market day. He dropped us at the bottom of John Street in New Guinea. We hadn't had time to tell anybody we were coming home. It was about half past eleven and as I walked up the street I could hear singing coming from our house. My dad was a violinist and he was playing as it was Christmas Eve. The house was full of relatives and neighbours. I just inched the door open, took my steel helmet from my epaulette and threw it under the table. That stopped all the singing. No-one got to bed before five o'clock the next morning.

Private Tommy Oughton, Barnsley Pals

By the time the demobilisation process had got fully under way, the euphoria of Armistice Day had worn off. Men who had marched away in the first days of war came home in 1919 to a grim reality:

There were no heroes' welcomes when we came back home. You couldn't expect it. There were so many men killed. They told me there wasn't one house that hadn't had a man killed or wounded, and the biggest part of them were colliers.

Private Ossie Burgess, 14th York and Lancasters

The war had almost bankrupted the country and the promised land, fit for heroes to live in, was just a dream. The comradeship that had helped them survive the trenches now helped them survive peace.

I, along with other men, started to look for work – but it was fruitless. I went back to Bradford, and I was out of work there for three years. I tried everything and anything – postal work – a course in motoring. But it was all fruitless – there were too many people, and drivers were ten a penny. We were queuing up at the labour exchange, but there were no jobs there for us – all they could do was hand out unemployment pay, which was eighteen shillings a week.

I was back and living at home, but drawing unemployment pay went down very badly with me. I suppose I didn't feel so badly about there being no jobs – I'd got away from the war, so even if life wasn't good, it was far better than the mud fields of Flanders. We were all in similar circumstances, so we just carried on.

At that time there was a government scheme, whereby they would allow a certain sum of money to any employer who took on an ex-serviceman for training. Eventually I sat down at a tailor's board and started learning the trade. In the summertime there was plenty of tailoring work, although in the winter it was a bit patchy. I stayed because there was no prospect of anything else. I learned to make clothes and just carried on. Eventually I got married and brought up a family and it was a case of sticking to one's trade. It was all right until the Second World War began, and with that work fell off dramatically. I managed to get a job in a wool warehouse – it was just labouring work – and that was where I was until I retired.

I hadn't given any deep thought to my future when I joined the army. For me it was a case of joining up to get away from the drab life of being on one's own in a little brick building and just serving men as they left with their loads of stuff for the mills and the gasworks. Life in the army promised more variety – more going on. After the war was over it gave me pause to look back and consider all the lives that had been sacrificed. It made me feel that, if there was such a thing, and if I was to be called up to serve in another war, I would certainly take a stand as a Christian man and come out dead against any service where men are compelled to fight. I never became an active pacifist after the war – besides, I was middle aged by the next war so I wasn't approached to fight again.

Private George Grunwell 16th Battalion, West Yorkshire Regiment

During the war, women volunteers tended graveyards behind the lines and acted as guides for those grieving parents able to make the journey to France. Many stayed on after the war to help with the influx of battlefield pilgrims.

In the middle of Baildon is a small wooden shack selling sweets. Embedded in the tarmac below it are small wheels. It was built by the local veterans association to provide work for a former soldier, the wheels making it mobile and therefore not subject to paying rates to the council. Nearby stand Lens Dive, Merville Avenue, Menin Drive, Hazebrouck Drive and St Eloi Close, all housing built on land purchased by the veterans to provide home for their colleagues. Ex-servicemen's clubs sprang up in every town where veterans could gather and talk to other men who understood what had happened in the trenches:

No they couldn't understand, I dare not tell them, the people at home couldn't begin to understand.

G. Denis, Hull, served in the King's Royal Rifle Corps

Veterans were unable to explain their experiences and families at home struggled to adjust to the trauma of the war years. Grief would haunt the streets of Yorkshire for generations to come:

[My mother] was struck dumb and dressed in black for many weeks after [the death of her son [Ernest]. The curtains in the house were never open and she would sit in darkness, never being the same again.

Olive Weasenham, Hull

On 7 November 1919, a year after the guns fell silent, King George issued a personal appeal:

Tuesday next, November 11, is the first anniversary of the Armistice, which stayed the world-wide carnage of the four preceding years and marked the victory of Right and Freedom. I believe that my people in every part of the Empire fervently wish to perpetuate the memory of the Great Deliverance. And of those who have laid down their lives to achieve it. To afford an opportunity for the universal expression of this feeling it is my desire and hope that at the hour when the Armistice came into force, the eleventh hour of the eleventh day of the eleventh month, there may be for the brief space of two minutes a complete suspension of all our normal activities. At a given signal ... I believe that we shall all gladly interrupt our business and pleasure ... and unite in this simple service of Silence and Remembrance.

He must have a strangely cold heart who was not moved by the impressive scenes witnessed yesterday. As eleven o'clock drew near there was a certain hesitancy in the movements in the streets. The centre of the city was thronged but, at the signal, immediately men uncovered their heads and women bowed their faces and all stood silently until the two minutes had passed.

Yorkshire Post, 12 November 1919

A century has passed since young men flocked to answer Kitchener's call and those who remembered the war are no longer around. The war has passed from living memory into the pages of history but in March 2014, two workmen digging at an industrial site near Ypres were killed when a Great War shell exploded. Each year the 'iron harvest' of munitions that have lain dormant since the war claim ever more victims. The last death as a result of the First World War has yet to happen.

As the anniversary of the war approaches, thousands of schoolchildren, not much younger than the men whose graves they visit, make the trip to France to remember ancestors they never knew. The cemeteries and scars of old trench lines mark the course of the Western Front and museums try to tell the story of what happened there.

But the land belongs to the men whose lives would be forever part of that foreign field:

It was the biggest incident in my life. I've lived sixty years afterwards and I've never got over it. It's always been there in my mind. It was the biggest thing that ever happened to me…When I go back there I feel I'm on consecrated ground. That ground has been trod by all those lovely lads who never came back. I think of that poem:

'They shall grow not old, as we that are left grow old: Age shall not weary them, nor the years condemn. At the going down of the sun and in the morning, we will remember them.'

I think it's marvellous. Because that's just how it is. You imagine them as they were then - not as they would be now – young, and in their prime, and never grown old.

Sergeant George Morgan, Bradford Pals

In war there will always be casualties, and it is the young and brave who are first to fall, the young and beautiful who are most likely to be killed … The importance of truth and love. That is what I had learnt, and is what I had to teach. It is the story I had to tell.

P. J. Campbell, West Riding Field Artillery

The real meaning of that comradeship was brought home to me when Grandpa died in 1974 at the grand old age of eighty-two. At his funeral I was surprised and touched to see a contingent of Pals (by then in their eighties) stood to attention outside the crematorium. They then did a smart right turn and marched in to pay their last respects. This really was a 'Pals' Battalion in the true sense of the word.

Margaret Sudol, Leeds

And now, Grandchildren, I have come safely through the war – whole in mind and body. But there are hundreds of thousands of warriors – men and women – who have died or been mutilated in the service of ourselves and of those against whom we fought and whose families were left in sadness. What caused the war? Was it worth it? And yet there came another world war and other smaller wars. Can it be prevented? Differences of opinion – desires for something you have not got and the other person has are bound to arise. We cannot all be top-level politicians trying to settle the inequalities, hardships and sufferings that exist in the world. The religions of the world, and especially our own Christian religion teach us to care for others – 'Love one another' – and there are also organisations who acknowledge no religion but teach the same message. Perhaps it is the ordinary people of our own country and other countries who by their behavior and beliefs can build up an influence which will be powerful enough to persuade the leaders of the Nations to settle their disputes and differences in peaceful and God-like ways. You yourselves can help by thinking and caring for other people and by doing your own job in life to the very best of your ability – and may God be with you in your efforts.

Cecil M. Slack, East Yorkshire Regiment

Everyone came to terms with the war in their own way, some coped better than others. Last word perhaps should go to Sheffielder Philip Howe, one of the few survivors of his battalion's disastrous experience on the first day of the Somme. In later years he summed up the terror and horror of his war with the simple phlegmatism that is the hallmark of the true Yorkshireman:

July 1 1916 was the most interesting day of my life.

Lieutenant Philip Howe, Military Cross,
10th West Yorkshires

On a warm summer's evening, the breeze ripples the field in front of Sheffield Park. Birds sing in the trees that have regrown in Mark, Luke and John Copses. Peace has returned to the shattered battlefield and it's sometimes hard not to imagine, on the cusp of hearing, laughter and songs in broad Tyke accents. Somewhere, just out of sight but never out of mind, the Pals are marching still.

'Two years in the making, ten minutes in the destroying'.
Pals battalion graves, Serre.

SELECT BIBLIOGRAPHY

Regimental and Unit Histories:

Barnes, B. S., *This Righteous War* (Richard Netherwood Ltd, 1990).
Clayton, D., *From Pontefract to Picardy* (Tempus, 2004).
Gibson, R., and P. Oldfield, *Sheffield Pals* (Pen & Sword, 2010).
Johnson, M., *Saturday Soldiers* (Doncaster Museum Service, 2004).
Magnus, L., *West Riding Territorials in the Great War* (Kegan Paul Trench Trubner & Co., 1920).
Milner, L., *Leeds Pals* (Pen & Sword, 1991).
Raw, D., *Bradford Pals* (Pen & Sword Books, 2005).
Skirrow, F., *Massacre on the Marne*, (Pen & Sword, 2007).
Sparling, R., *History of the 12th (Service) Battalion, York & Lancaster Regiment* (J. W. Northend, 1920).
Wyrall, E., *The History of the 62nd (West Riding) Division 1914-1919*, (Bodley Head, 1928).

Local Histories:

Johnson, M. K., *Surely we are Winning?* (Propagator Press, 2007).
Lee, J. A., *Todmorden in the Great War* (Waddington, 1922).
Lomax, S., *Home Front: Sheffield in the Great War*

(Pen & Sword, 2014).

Woods, M. & Platts, T., *Bradford in the Great War* (Sutton Publishing, 2007).

Peacock, A. J., *York in the Great War* (York Settlement Trust, 1993).

Pearce, C., *Comrades in Conscience* (Francis Boutle, 2001).

Scott, W. H., *Leeds in the Great War* (Leeds Libraries and Arts Committee, 1923).

Shepherd, T., *Kingston-Upon-Hull Before, During and After the Great War*, (A. Brown & Sons, 1919).

Local Newspapers:

Bradford Telegraph
Halifax Courier
Harrogate Herald
Huddersfield Daily Examiner
Huddersfield Weekly Examiner
Hull Daily Mail
Pontefract and Castleford Express
The Worker
York Herald
Yorkshire Observer
Yorkshire Post

Memoirs:

Campbell, P. J., *Refuge From Fear*, (Hamish Hamilton, 1982).

Justus, H., *An Unconducted Tour of England. In Escapers All* (Bodley Head, 1932).

Pearce, E., *Through the Camp Sewer. In Escapers All* (Bodley Head, 1932).

Priestley, J. B., *Margin Released* (Bookprint Ltd, 1962).

Priestman, E. Y., *With a B. P. Scout in Gallipoli*, (George Routledge & Sons, 1916).

Sachsse, S., & R. Cossmann, *Kriegsgefangen in Skipton* (Ernst Reinhart, 1920).

Slack, C. M., *Grandfather's* Adventure, (Arthur Stockwell, 1977).

Spicer, L., *Letters From France*, (Robert York, 1979).

INDEX

PLACES

Africa   11, 45, 166
Barnsley   33/34, 39-42, 58,
61, 65, 79-82, 103–4, 105,
106/07, 114, 122, 124, 132–3,
137-39, 146-49, 158, 160,
167, 173, 193, 202, 205
Beverley   12, 153
Bradford   12, 13, 18, 36, 39,
40, 41–2, 53, 56, 58–9, 63,
67, 72–3, 103–7, 109, 122,
125, 127–9, 130–6, 139, 149–
50, 175, 203, 205–6, 209
Colsterdale   68, 80, 197
Dewsbury   11, 54, 201
Doncaster   84–5, 91, 199
Egypt   94, 103, 105-7, 112,
122, 123, 128, 167
Goole   9, 11, 91, 153, 154
Halifax   12, 28-30, 35, 60, 86,
109
Huddersfield   11, 18, 20, 27,

30, 53, 73, 109–10, 113–14,
116, 118
Hull   11, 12, 17, 28, 33, 48–9,
53, 55–8, 91–2, 93, 98, 103,
111, 122–5, 140, 144-7,
152–5, 201, 208
India   30, 35, 104, 107, 164,
167
Keighley   32, 36-8, 42, 91, 112-
13, 173, 195
Leeds   12, 15, 17, 19–20, 49-
53, 56, 57-72, 78, 79, 80-82,
85-86, 88, 91, 103–4, 105,
108–9, 112–13, 122-25, 127,
129–30, 131, 132, 135-36,
142, 148, 150, 151, 154,
158–9, 174-76, 178, 184, 189,
190, 194, 200–2, 205, 210
Malta   84, 101, 105, 169–70
Middlesbrough   12, 192
Pontefract   12, 119, 155–9
Russia   20-22, 33–4, 53, 93–4,
119–20, 164, 170-9, 189
Salonica   169

NAMES

GENERAL INDEX

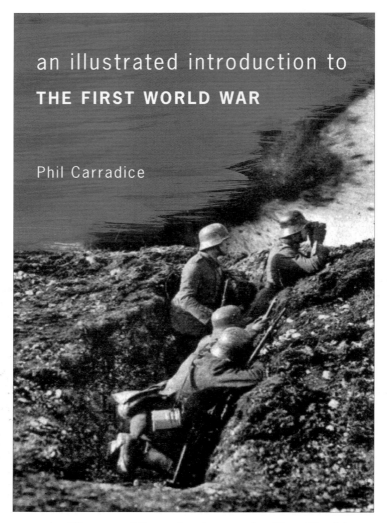

An Illustrated Introduction to the First World War
Phil Carradice

This fascinating selection of photographs traces the events of the
First World War and those that fought in it.

978 1 4456 3296 4
96 pages, full colour

1914: The First World War in Photographs:
John Christopher and Campbell McCutcheon

1914: the first year of the 'war to end all wars', documented through old photographs.

978 1 4456 2181 4
96 pages, full colour

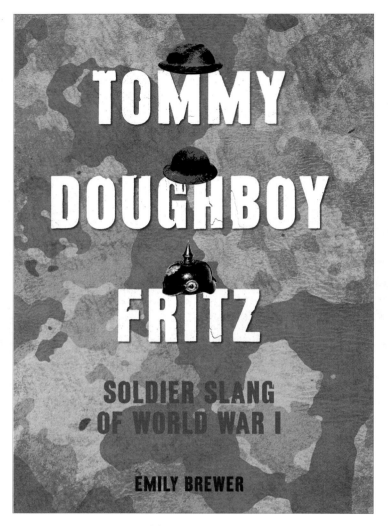

Yorkshire's Three Peaks:
The Inside Story of the Dales
Mike Appleton
The Three Peaks of Yorkshire – Ingleborough, Pen-y-ghent and
Whernside – hold a unique fascination and focal point for all who
head to the Dales. Using the famous Three Peaks Walk as a road
map, Mike Appleton takes a tour around this most popular of areas
and finds the real story of the picturesque Dales.

978 1 4456 0487 9
160 pages

Available from all good bookshops or order direct
from our website www.amberleybooks.com

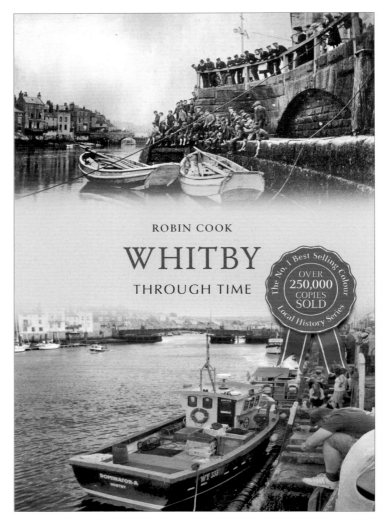